# How to Write

# Effective Reports

# How to Write Effective Reports

*Programed by*  FEDERAL ELECTRIC CORPORATION

ADDISON-WESLEY PUBLISHING COMPANY, INC.
READING, MASSACHUSETTS

Addison-Wesley Publishing Company, Inc.

*Headquarters:*
  Reading, Massachusetts 01867

*School Division Office:*
  3220 Porter Drive, Palo Alto, California 94304

*Sales Office:*
  411 Elm Street, Dallas, Texas 75202

*Sales Office:*
  10–15 Chitty Street, London W1, England

# Preface

This book is arranged in a way that may not be familiar to you; the arrangement is based on a new learning technique called "programed instruction." As you work your way through the text, you will discover these features of programed instruction:

1. You work by yourself, at your own speed.

2. You take an active part in the learning process. Instead of passively reading text material, you have frequent opportunities all along the way to prove to yourself that you have learned.

3. You learn a small amount of material—usually a single fact or principle—at a time. Whereas the ordinary textbook has perhaps twenty questions at the end of a thirty-page chapter, the programed text contains questions interspersed throughout the chapter; thus you may be sure you have mastered each fact before you proceed to the next.

Most of the material in this book is presented in the following way: Having read two or three paragraphs of material, you will be asked a question. You will select the best answer from several choices provided. A page reference accompanies each choice, and you will turn to the page indicated for the answer you selected. If your answer was the correct one, you will be so informed and will go on to new material. If you choose a wrong answer, your mistake will be corrected, and you will be sent back to the question page to make another selection.

You will notice that the information in this book is not presented sequentially in page-number order—the answer page may be before or after the question page. The important thing to remember is to proceed through the book strictly according to the instructions that appear on each page.

It would be nice, of course, if you could go through the entire book without selecting any wrong answers. But there is nothing wrong with making mistakes. The special advantage of programed instruction is that your mistakes are corrected immediately, and you learn the correct answer before proceeding to new material.

We say that you can work at your own speed. But we make this reservation—don't try to do too much at a time. Complete a chapter or part of a chapter, then take a break. You will work much better when you are fresh.

Now go to page 3 and start the program.

Good luck!

# Acknowledgments

This project was under the general direction of O. Wolf, Manager, Special Services Department and C. G. Latterner, Manager, Training.

The instructional material and text were prepared by D. Martin and J. Gumbinger of the Special Services Department's Training Branch. Engineering and Support Services Division, under the supervision of G. Uslan.

# Contents

# Introduction

How many times yesterday did you issue, or receive, a report? Before you answer, maybe we'd better define our term: A report is the communication of information to someone who wants or needs it, in the most convenient and usable form.

On that basis, do you number yesterday's reports in the tens—or the hundreds? When we communicate, we report. In addition to the high school student's book report and the businessman's progress report, we have the homecoming husband's report of his day at the office, his wife's report on their child's behavior and the icebox breakdown, the baby's loud report on the fact that dinner should be served, Aunt Helen's postcard report on the fine weather in Burmuda, the TV news-of-the-day report, which happens to include the President's report to the nation on the international situation, and so on, and on, and on.

Most of the reports that you are concerned with in your everyday affairs are of the oral variety. You prepare and issue them without much thought; and, just as quickly, you interpret the reports that come to you and file the information away in your brain. The reports that we will deal with in this book, however, are of the more substantial kind. We mean the reports that you are required to present in writing, either as a part of your schooling or as a part of your job. In theory, these reports have the same job as the casual oral reports: they communicate information to someone, in a form he will find usable. But there is a lot more pressure on you when you go about preparing a written report. The student worries about his grades; the worker worries about his job.

We intend in this programed course in report writing to teach you what you need to know to write a satisfactory report—how to select the type of report that will present your information best, what information you should include to meet the requirements of a given assignment, and how to write your report in a style that is readable, interesting, and correct.

One thing you will learn is that reports are grouped in two ways:

1. Into three classes by format (appearance and size): the informal, the semiformal, and the formal.

2. Into three types by function: the informational, the analytical, and the special.

As you proceed through the course, you will find out how to select the type and class of report that will best accomplish the particular job you have to do.

Julius Caesar wrote the report that, if it isn't the shortest, must be the best remembered: *"Veni, vidi, vici"*—"I came, I saw, I conquered." He didn't go into detail, but it was a very effective reporting job. Typically, a report condenses information into brief form. It presents, for instance, a 500-word summary of the activities of a department for a week, or a 2000-word description of the results of a two-month investigation. We defined a report as the communication of information to someone, in the most convenient and usable form. We should add that "convenience" includes speed. A good report will permit the reader (the audience) to get the message *quickly*.

Many factors contribute to how quickly the audience will get the message—selection and organization of material, choice of language, use of visual aids in presentation of data, etc. You will find, in this course, a good deal of information on how to put these factors to work for you.

In the preceding paragraphs we've introduced you to some of the things you will learn about writing reports. Now go to page 7 and begin your studies by reading about the basic factor that shapes every report—the audience.

# 1

The Audience
Shapes the Report

When you begin to write a report, the first thing you should think about is the audience—the individual or group who will read the report and use the material it contains. We defined a report as conveying information "to someone who wants or needs it." The key word in the definition is "someone." Knowing your audience, you have a basis for making decisions all along the line, including decisions on the length of the report, the format, the writing style, the comprehension level, and so on. As an obvious example, if your subject were "This Year at Apex Rubber," a report aimed at the production workers would read quite differently from a report to the stockholders.

Knowing the audience also includes knowing how the report will be used. The report you send to a clerk will enable him to bring records up to date, and the report to your boss may help him reach a decision, whereas a report to the company executive committee may be used just for general information.

Here's the situation: It's your first week on the job, and you've been asked to write about five pages describing your reactions to the way you were welcomed into the company. What is the first thing you would do?

1. Select a report format.    **Page 11**
2. Determine who will receive the report.    **Page 13**
3. Outline the material to be covered.    **Page 15**

*The term "audience" refers to a person or a group, not to the report's purpose.*

No, I'm afraid you're wrong. Audience *does* include purpose.

Go back to page 13, select the other answer, and you'll find out exactly why.

*A report to a shipping foreman of a firm in Hong Kong, giving details about an incomplete delivery.*

We don't think you mean that. Just consider: your audience is halfway around the world, and you don't even know whether he can speak English. You can list the items that weren't received, but you may need a translator to get your message across.

Go back to page 10 and try again.

*The term "audience" includes the purpose of the report—the use to which it will be put.*

We agree. Here's why: we could, of course, state the purpose of a report merely by saying, for instance, that a "product report" evaluates a product, and a "process report" describes a process. But really these are just titles; they define the purpose only very generally.

Basically, *all reports have the same purpose.* By our definition, they "convey information to someone who *wants or needs* it." The question is, who is the someone, *and for what purpose* does he want or need the report? It's that someone, your audience, who shapes your report from outline through format selection to finished job. Once you have a clear picture of him—who he is and how he will use the report—you can begin devising ways to convey information to him.

Which would be the easiest to write?

1. A report to your new boss, analyzing an equipment failure.   **Page 20**
2. A note to your girlfriend, giving travel directions.   **Page 16**
3. A report to a shipping foreman of a firm in Hong Kong, giving details about an incomplete delivery.   **Page 9**

*Select a report format.*

Well, selecting a format is important, but you're doing it too early in the game. On page 7 we discussed the one factor that is really basic to all others.

Go back to page 7 and make another selection.

**12**

*The audience of my report will always be an individual.*

You're wrong, but we wish you were right. The report writer's life would be an easier one if every report were aimed at one individual. But we're afraid there's more to it than that.

Go back to page 16 and make the other selection.

*Determine who will receive the report.*

Right you are! *Audience* is the basic factor.

You will find that most of your reports are directed at an individual. Who he is and how he will use your report are vital to your approach. Even if you don't know him personally, try to establish a clear picture of him in your mind: What's his job? How familiar is he with your subject? How much time can he devote to it? Does he need to be filled in on some background information or have terms defined? How will he use the report? The more you know about your audience, the better your report will be.

Which is the better statement?

1. The term "audience" includes the purpose of the report—the use to which it will be put.   **Page 10**
2. The term "audience" refers to a person or a group, not to the report's purpose.   **Page 8**

**14**

FROM PAGE 16

*I should consider the fact that my report may be used by more than one audience.*

Very good. You foresaw one of the report writer's big problems: *the secondary audience.* That fellow we've talked about so far is the *immediate audience,* and he's usually not hard to identify. The secondary audence can be elusive. It may be one person, or 100. He may know a great deal about your subject, or nothing. He may use your report next month, or pull it out of a file two years from now. But unless your report is so simple that anybody could understand it, or so complex that nobody could, you have to give the secondary audience some thought.

First, find out if there will be a secondary audence. Assuming there is, what is the best way to write the report?

1. Write the report so that it will be useful to both audiences. **Page 22**
2. Aim at the immediate audience, and let the secondary audience pick up what it can.     **Page 17**
3. Aim at the secondary audience, to be sure that everyone gets something out of the report.     **Page 19**

*Outline the material to be covered.*

No, that isn't the best way to do the job. Outlines are invaluable aids to organization, and you will want to prepare one. But there's a more basic consideration, which we discussed on page 7.

Go back to page 7 and make another choice.

*A note to your girl friend, giving travel directions.*

Correct. And why? Because you know just how much information to give. You know whether she has a good sense of direction and whether she's been in the general area before. You shape your instructions accordingly.

In the same way, the language you use in your report is also shaped by the audience. If you can't put your information into terms he can understand, there will be no communication. Furthermore, audience determines format. It's not just knowing the facts that counts, it's knowing how to present the facts. This may not matter so much in memos and short, informal reports, but it's vital in semi-formal and formal reports, whose audience may be your boss or your boss's boss. (We'll talk more about this in the next chapter.) Does *he* like long reports, or short ones? Does he prefer a summary at the beginning, or at the end? Would he rather that you just supply the facts and leave the decision-making up to him, or does he want recommendations from you?

Which of the following would you agree with?

1. The audience of my report will always be an individual.
   **Page 12**
2. I should consider the fact that my report may be used by more than one audience.   **Page 14**

*Aim at the immediate audience, and let the secondary audience pick up what it can.*

I'm afraid not. That would really leave the secondary audience out in the cold. We may not know who he is, but usually he'll be there, so we should make some attempt to communicate with him.

Go back to page 14 and try again.

*Consider the man at the top to be the immediate audience.*

You're right. Since he is the man who will ultimately make decisions based on your report, naturally he is the primary target. The reviewers at lower levels are really a secondary audience, in spite of the fact that they see the report first.

Often your entire report won't get to the top man—only a part of it will. What happens here is called the "pyramid effect." Look again at page 23. The effect works this way: Each supervisor who reports to the Plant Superintendent receives progress reports from three foremen. He combines the important parts of these three reports and submits his own report to the Superintendent. The Superintendent, in turn, combines the important parts of the supervisors' reports, and submits the result to the Works Manager. So an idea from your report may make it all the way to the top of the pyramid—the General Manager (but he'll never know it came from you).

Which statement do you agree with?

**1.** The pyramid effect involves fragments, not complete reports.
**Page 27**
**2.** The pyramid effect involves complete reports.     **Page 25**

*Aim at the secondary audience, to be sure that everyone gets something out of the report.*

That's a nice, safe approach, but what happens to your immediate audience? He's still our number one worry. He may not have time to dig through a lot of background information that he doesn't need before he gets to the point.

Go back to page 14 and make another selection.

*A report to your new boss, analyzing an equipment failure.*

Maybe you can adjust to a new situation more quickly than most people. Maybe you're astute enough to know just how much detail your new boss expects, and what style of presentation he likes. But, honestly now, wouldn't you be a little uncertain about that first assignment?

Go back to page 10 and make another selection.

*Consider the first man who will see the report to be the immediate audience, those who follow as secondary.*

No good. Suppose the first reviewer was your supervisor, and he had some familiarity with the subject. If you assumed that he was your immediate audience, you would leave out some information that the decision-making executive would need.

Go back to page 24 and make another selection.

*Write the report so that it will be useful to both audiences.*

Right! It's obvious that a report is better if it can be used by several people, rather than just one. Of course, this isn't always possible. But if, by adding a page of definitions or by referring the reader to an outside source, you can broaden the usefulness of your report, by all means do it.

To sum up:

1. Find out all you can about your immediate audience.

2. Find out if there is a secondary audience, and whatever details are available about it.

Part of knowing the audience is knowing where he is, and how the report will travel in getting to him. Take a look at the illustration on page 23. The dashed line shows a report traveling "horizontally" from a production line supervisor to the Administrator of the Receiving Department, reporting faulty materials. A report from the Administrator of Production Control to the Works Manager travels "vertically" up the chain of command.

Usually reports that travel horizontally are short and simple— memos, informal reports, and the like. In most cases they have only an immediate audience, and are so simple that, if filed, they could be understood by anyone who might have the need. Quite the reverse is true of vertically directed reports. Very often they are semiformal or formal in construction, and have a secondary audience.

*(Continued on page 24.)*

23

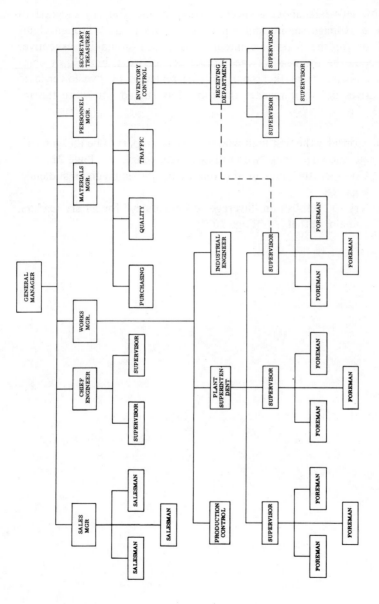

PANEL 1-1

**24**

Now let's talk about a special case. Suppose you are assigned to write a 10-page semiformal report which has to go "through channels" or "up the chain of command" to a decision-making executive. (He could be the head of the department, division, branch, or company.) Assume that the report will be reviewed by five lower-level executives before it reaches the top. How should you write the report?

1. Consider the first man who will see the report to be the immediate audience, those who follow as secondary. **Page 21**
2. Consider the man at the top to be the immediate audience. **Page 18**
3. Try to establish an "average of immediacy" for all six readers, and aim at that. **Page 26**

*The pyramid effect involves complete reports.*

We don't think you were paying attention. The pyramid effect occurs when ideas or facts from several reports are combined into a single report, and this process is repeated at a succession of administrative levels. If the entire report were being forwarded, you would just think of the top man as the immediate audience.

Go back to page 18 and make the other selection.

*Try to establish an "average of immediacy" for all six readers, and aim at that.*

You're wrong on two counts:

1. This kind of average would be just about impossible to determine, or at least very time-consuming. Think about it.

2. Even if you could establish an average, the very fact that it *was* an average would make everybody a secondary audience. And we always must have an immediate audience in mind.

Go back to page 24 and try again.

*The pyramid effect involves fragments, not complete reports.*

Right. Good work. That completes our discussion of audience.

Now for a little review: Look at the organization chart on page 23.

Harry Morgan, from the Plant Superintendent's office, writes a 10-page report describing a new system for speeding up the service at coffee breaks. His supervisor, Mr. Harris, reads it and passes it along to the three supervisors of assembly-line departments for their comments. Later, Mr. Harris writes his own report, including parts of Harry Morgan's report as well as some of the supervisors' comments. He forwards this report to the Works Manager.

Complete these statements:

1. Mr. Harris is Harry Morgan's _____ audience.

2. The three supervisors are the _____ audience.

3. The report that Mr. Harris wrote, using some of Harry Morgan's data, is an example of the. . .

4. When Mr. Harris wrote his report, his immediate audience was the. . .

Go to page 28.

1. *immediate;* 2. *secondary;* 3. *pyramid effect;* 4. *Works Manager.*

If you missed question 1, 2, or 4, go back to page 14 and start from there.

If you missed question 3, start again from page 18.

If you answered all the questions correctly, congratulations. Turn to page 31 and begin work on Chapter 2.

# Report Format

Most reports contain six basic parts or modifications of these six parts. The parts are:

1. Introduction
2. Summary
3. Body

4. Conclusions
5. Recommendations
6. Appendix

A pictorial representation of the order in which the parts of the report will usually be presented, and the proportion of the report that will usually be devoted to each part, is shown in the diagram below.

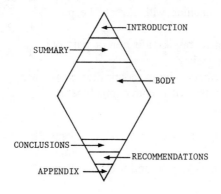

In the introduction, the writer tells the reader the purpose of the report. In the summary, the writer sums up the complete report. In some short reports, the introduction and summary are combined into one section, but in long formal reports they will always be separate sections. The body of a report is the portion in which the facts and details are presented. The writer will draw conclusions based upon the facts presented in the body of the report. The conclusions must be based upon the information presented in the body, not upon other information, not stated in the report. The recommendations, in turn, will be based upon the conclusions, and will offer some solution if the report is of a problem-solving nature. The final part of the report is the appendix, which is used to display detailed data that is not immediately needed in the body of the report. Information such as reference tables of statistics are presented in the appendix.

*(Continued on page 32.)*

Not all reports will always contain all six parts. The format is completely flexible, and can be modified as necessary to suit a situation.

Match the short statements below with the part of the report into which they will be placed.

1. All information points to the need for a coffee machine.
2. The coffee machine must fit into a space no larger than $6' \times 4' \times 4'$.
3. This report will give the reasons why a coffee machine will have to be purchased.
4. Since coffee breaks are now a part of company policy . . .
5. The members of this committee suggest that the Jiffy coffee machine be purchased.

A. Introduction

B. Summary

C. Body

D. Conclusions

E. Recommendations

F. Appendix

**1.** 1-E, 2-D, 3-B, 4-C, and 5-E.     **Page 38**
**2.** 1-D, 2-C, 3-A, 4-C, and 5-E.     **Page 42**
**3.** 1-D, 2-D, 3-A, 4-A, and 5-D.     **Page 37**

*Number 2 is not an informal report.*

Well, if it isn't an informal report, what is it? It's short, the writing style would be best classified as informal (don't you agree?)—and we specifically mentioned that "brief handwritten notes" would be classified as informal reports. Maybe you'd better review the material on page 34, and then select the correct answer on page 35.

Now that you know the general format for reports, you're ready for the types of reports. The most common of these is the informal report. Its identifying characteristic is length: informal reports are *short,* usually one or two pages. Memos, letter reports, and brief handwritten notes telling someone of routine activities are all classified as informal reports, even though they may be only one paragraph long. Informal reports that are more than one page long will follow the general report format, often in shortened form. They will have an introduction-summary, a body section to present the facts, and a conclusions-recommendations section at the end.

Memos are a common type of informal report used in business. The style or format for the memo is usually set by company or department policy, but all memos will contain four essential items of information. They are: (1) the date, (2) the addressee, (3) the sender, and (4) the subject of the memo.

MEMORANDUM

June 15, 1970

To:        All Department Managers

From:      Engineering Department Manager

Subject:   Report of Engineering Department
           Meeting, June 14, 1970

The letter report will contain the same four essential elements that a memo has, but, as the name implies, the format of an ordinary business letter is used. Both the memo and the letter report will only be used for short informal reports that would only cover a single topic or subject.

*(Continued on page 35.)*

Which of the following is not an informal report?

**1.** A seven-page report on the first 12 weeks of project X.

**Page 45**

**2.**

*January 21, 1964*

*Bob,*

*About that purchase order #0735, have your girl retype it with the new figures and I will O.K. it.*

*Dave*

**Page 33**

**3.**

January 21, 1964

To:        J. K. Bean

From:      J. Smith

Subject:     Widgets

     Our supply of widgets is...

**Page 47**

*The six parts of the basic report format are:*

Introduction
Summary
Body
Conclusions
Recommendations
Appendix

If you answered correctly go to page 34. If not, study the names of the six parts until you can write them from memory. Then go to page 34.

*1-D, 2-D, 3-A, 4-A, and 5-D.*

Sorry, but you have made three mistakes.

1. Statement 2, "The coffee machine must fit into a space no larger than 6′ × 4′ ×4′," cannot be in the conclusions portion of the report unless the report is dealing with only the size of the machine.

2. Statement 4, "Since coffee breaks are now a part of company policy . . ." would not be a part of the introduction because it does not tell what the report is about. (However, it *could* be the opening sentence in the body of the report.)

3. Statement 5, "The members of this committee suggest that the Jiffy coffee machine be purchased," would not be in the conclusions part of the report because it is suggesting something, rather than drawing some conclusions from the facts presented in the body of the report.

Now return to page 31, reread that page and then make another selection on page 32.

**38**

*1-E, 2-D, 3-B, 4-C, and 5-E.*

Sorry, but you have made a few mistakes in your choice.

1. The statement, "All information points to the need for a coffee machine," is not a recommendation. A recommendation will usually say something like, "It is suggested (or advised, or recommended) that the following action be taken."

2. "The coffee machine must fit into a space no larger than 6' × 4' × 4'." This statement cannot be in the conclusions portion of the report unless the report deals with only the size of the machine.

3. "This report will give the reasons why a coffee machine will have to be purchased." By stretching it a bit we just might be able to call this part of the summary, but rather than summing up the report, don't you think this statement tells what the report is about?

Now return to page 31, reread that page and then make another selection on page 32.

*A report from a supervisor to a manager on the reasons why he needs
to add six men to his work force.*

Right you are! We're talking about a move that will cost the company up to $30,000 a year in salaries alone. Our supervisor will
have to take considerable pains to justify the expense. The semiformal report will do the job best.

The last report format we'll talk about is the formal. This type has
two identifying features:

1. *Its appearance.* The informal report can be handwritten or typewritten, and seldom will copies be made. If copies are made (for instance: a memo from the manager to all employees asking for more
promptness in reporting to work), the reproduction job will be cheap
—ditto, or at best mimeograph. The semiformal report will be typewritten; again, copies, if necessary, will be made cheaply—ditto,
mimeograph, or some comparable process usually suffices. On the
other hand, the formal report is intended for an audience that may
be large (for example, the stockholders' report, or a sales brochure)
or else small but important (for example, a report to the company
board of directors). But any report that has the appearance of expensive reproduction—an expensive three-ring binder, multicolor printing, coated paper, illustrations, a high-quality printing job—can be
assumed to be a formal report.

2. *Its volume.* A report that contains all six parts of the report
format, that runs to more than 15 pages, and that deals with a subject worthy of the formal approach, is a formal report. It does not
necessarily have to be expensively reproduced.

As a rule of thumb, we can say that if a report is (a) big, or (b) expensively reproduced, or both, it is a formal report. Panel 2–3 (next
page) is a typical cover for a formal report.

*(Continued on page 41.)*

**40**

# INSTRUCTION IN
# PROGRAMED LEARNING
# TECHNIQUES

 FEDERAL ELECTRIC CORPORATION

Which of the following subjects would you rate worthy of formal treatment?

1. A report of the results of a statistical analysis of changing urban and rural population patterns, to be circulated among sociology professors at major universities as part of a textbook sales program.

2. A proposal to a U.S. Government agency, describing a firm's experience and capabilities in a given area, in an attempt to land a contract.

3. A report to the company president, describing the progress made during the past two years on construction of a new building for the company's Denver office.

4. A report to the department manager, analyzing the extent to which a newly acquired machine has improved production in terms of quantity and quality.

**1.** Numbers 1 and 4.      **Page 52**
**2.** Numbers 1, 2, and 3.      **Page 48**
**3.** All of them.      **Page 50**

*1-D, 2-C, 3-A, 4-C, and 5-E.*

You are correct in your selections. Although a change in emphasis on the subject of the report might put some of the items in other parts of the report, the selections you made represent the best way to arrange the given statements.

Now list the six parts of the basic report format in their proper order, and check your answer on page 36.

*A report from a foreman to a supervisor, explaining 10 minutes'*
*"down" time on No. 3 machine.*

No, we'd better take another look at the situation. We're talking about 10 minutes of machine time, and our report is traveling in the lower echelons of management. Now, if that report is five pages long, either the machine had something pretty strange happen to it (and if it did, who fixed it in just 10 minutes?), or else your foreman is to be suspected of making a mountain out of a molehill. On second thought, wouldn't you agree that 10 minutes' "down" time could better be reported informally?

Go back to page 45 and make another selection.

**PANEL 2–1**

MEMORANDUM

June 15, 1964

To:           All Department Managers

From:         Engineering Department Manager

Subject:      Report of Engineering Department
              Meeting, June 14, 1964

The branch managers of the Engineering Department
met with me to discuss possible improved methods
of organizing Engineering activities.

Several innovations were mentioned, among them a
proposal to reorganize the structure of the draft-
ing group. Mr. Hennessy, Electrical Engineering
branch manager, suggested that a committee be
formed to determine what costs would be saved by
such a reorganization.

The committee was formed, composed of Mr. Hennessy,
Mr. Johnson, and Mr. Thompson. They will report
their findings in two weeks.

T. J. Sullivan

                           T. J. Sullivan

*Number 1 is not an informal report.*

Right! It fails to meet the qualifications of an informal report on two counts: it's more than five pages long, and its scope (the first 12 weeks of Project X) takes it out of the classification of "routine activities."

We mentioned three informal report formats—memos, letters, and notes (which are simply memos without the heading). A sample memo appears in Panel 2–1 (opposite page), a sample letter report in Panel 2–2 (page 46). For a sample note, just picture the memo without its heading.

The second classification of report format is the semiformal. Semiformal reports can be identified in three ways:

1. *Length.* They are longer than informal reports, ranging from 5 to 15 pages.

2. *Subject matter.* (a) They are broader in scope than informal reports. They cover such topics as a week's activities in a department or section, a comparison of accident rates for the past two years, an inquiry into the most feasible way to improve the finish on a machined part—subjects that require some research or investigation, and several hours' preparation time.

(b) And, for the most part, semiformal reports are written on subjects that are of interest to persons inside the company, rather than outside.

Which of the following subjects would be handled in a semiformal report?

1. An annual report to stockholders.    **Page 49**
2. A report from a foreman to a supervisor, explaining 10 minutes' "down" time on No. 3 machine.    **Page 43**
3. A report from a supervisor to a manager on the reasons why he needs to add six men to his work force.    **Page 39**

**PANEL 2–2**

Al Simmons, Field Engineer
Lucky Streak Mine
c/o General Delivery
Hog Wallow, Wyoming

Mr. Henry Field, Supervisory Engineer
Merton Metal Company
Fort Allen, Pennsylvania

Dear Mr. Field:

This is my report for the week of August 14.

In general, the progress with the work is completely satisfactory, and remains slightly ahead of schedule.

As you know, we are making 36 test drillings. During the week ending as of second shift Friday, completed 6, and the total completed is now 23. Samplings from the six new wells were mailed to the home office this morning. Nothing, it appears, will get in the way of our completing the job slightly in advance of the September 5 deadline.

Once again, everything is in good shape.

Sincerely,

*Al Simmons*

Al Simmons,
Field Engineer

*Number 3 is not an informal report.*

We thought that question was a giveaway. On page 34, you'll find a sample of the heading of a memorandum (which, you remember, is a type of informal report). Compare that sample with the heading in Number 3, page 35, then make the correct selection.

*Numbers 1, 2, and 3.*

Right. Number 4 is disqualified because it certainly would not be expensively reproduced, and almost certainly would not contain more than 15 pages.

Before we review, we'd like to offer a short comment on the material you learned in this chapter. As you probably noticed, it's virtually impossible to make any hard-and-fast rules about either report format or report types. It's always possible to find exceptions. For example, we said that a letter report was informal—but very often a consulting firm will report the results of its investigations in the form of a long letter, which will be in the semiformal classification. And sometime, somewhere, someone no doubt has sent out a memo with an appendix.

What we have tried to do, therefore, is to provide you with some guidelines to what kinds of subjects are treated in what kinds of reports, and to the section titles that you will use to organize your report. In the previous chapter, you learned that the audience shapes the report. With that in mind, you modify both the type and the format to suit the situation.

Now, a quick review:

1. Name the six parts of the general report format.
2. Name the three types of reports and give the identifying characteristics of each.

When you have written your answer, go to page 51.

*An annual report to stockholders.*

No, we would disqualify that one on two counts:

1. Unless you have in mind a very small corporation, the annual report will run more than 15 pages.
2. The semiformal report is directed inside the company. Stockholders are usually thought of as being outside the company.

(Actually, there is a third reason, which we'll come to in our discussion of formal reports.)

Go back to page 45 and make another selection.

*All of them.*

Well, you're partly right. Remember the yardsticks by which we measure "formality": large volume, or expensive appearance, or both. Not all of those reports fit that picture.

Go back to page 41 and make another selection.

1. *The general report format contains:*

   Introduction
   Summary
   Body
   Conclusions
   Recommendations
   Appendix

2. *The types of reports are:*

   Informal—short
   Semiformal—5 to 15 pages in length, fairly complex subject.
   Formal—expensive appearance, large size, or both.

   Go on to Chapter 3, page 55.

**52**

*Numbers 1 and 4.*

No, we'll have to disagree with you. You must not have studied the material on page 39 with quite enough attention. Rather than give you the right answers, we'll just ask you to review page 39 carefully, then make another selection on page 41.

# The Mechanics
# of Writing a Report

You've determined the audience of your report and selected the most suitable format. Looks as though you're about ready to start putting words on paper.

The first writing will be the preparation of an outline. Outlines are necessary in all but the most simple reports, and they will be an invaluable aid to you. No doubt you've worked with outlines before. As you may remember, they help in several ways:

1. They boil the data down to brief statements which can later be used as headings in your report; a sentence outline will provide main sentences for your paragraphs.

2. They indicate the relative importance of facts and the relationships between them.

3. From an outline you can easily prepare a summary.

4. You can have your outline approved before you go to the trouble of writing a complete report.

5. An outline helps you pick out and discard irrelevant facts.

Converting your notes from raw form into a logical outline can be tricky. Assuming you have all your data assembled, what do you think will be the most foolproof way to proceed?

1. Write the outline directly from the raw notes.     **Page 59**
2. Transfer the raw notes to 3 × 5-in. cards, one fact to a card. **Page 67**
3. Write the first draft of the report.     **Page 74**

**56**

*The skeleton style.*

This is the style you're probably most familiar with, and we recommend it for flexibility and ease of handling. Here's a more complete sample:

THE SECOND WORLD WAR

    I. The Naval Campaigns
       A. The Pacific Theater
          1. The Southwest Pacific
             a. The Battle of the Coral Sea
             b. The Battle of Savo Island
          2. The Central Pacific
             a. The Attack on Pearl Harbor
             b. The Battle of Midway
       B. The Atlantic Theater, etc.

   II. The Land Campaigns, etc.

From now on, when we talk about outlines, we will mean skeleton outlines.

Go to page 60.

*The decimal style.*

There isn't really any right or wrong answer to this question. You can use whatever outlining style suits you. The one advantage of the decimal style is that it can be used with or without indention. For this reason, it finds frequent use in Government manuals, and is especially useful when you get down to about the tenth level of subordination: 1. 3. 7. 2. 4. 4. 8. 9. 3. 1. If you were using the indent style, you would be all the way across the page. That's when it gets pretty confusing, too. The skeleton style is generally easier to handle, and unless you have a strong preference for the decimal style, you'll find the skeleton style best for most purposes. When we talk about outlines from now on, we'll be referring to skeleton outlines.

Go to page 60.

*The indent style.*

This is a fairly good style, with, however, a couple of drawbacks.

1. The differences between levels of subordination are not brought home quite as forcefully as they are when letters and numbers are used.

2. Unlike the skeleton style, the indent style makes it impossible to refer a reader quickly to a specific line—for instance, IV. A. 1. c.

Neither of these considerations applies to the skeleton style, and for this reason the skeleton style will be the better one for you to use. From now on, when we talk about outlines, we'll mean skeleton outlines.

Go to page 60.

*Write the outline directly from the raw notes.*

This is one way to do it, but not the best, especially for a 10-page report. You will almost certainly have to rewrite the outline a couple of times before you get the facts into the best order for presentation.

Go back to page 55 and make another selection.

We hope you've decided on the skeleton style as the best one to
use. (We were trying to sell you on it.)

Our next problem is major headings: What do we put next to
those roman numerals? It's easy. As you learned in Chapter 2, the
diamond-shaped report format breaks down into six major parts:
Introduction, Summary, Body, Conclusions, Recommendations, and
Appendixes. These are naturally suited to be the major divisions of
your outline.

Before we go any further, let's clear up a possible area of confusion: the difference between a general outline and a report outline.
The report outline contains at least some of the headings we just
mentioned; the general outline has no such limitations. When we ask
you to organize a set of facts into an outline, we mean a general outline, unless we specify otherwise.

What do you think about these propositions?

1. All reports will have all six basic sections, and in the same
   order.   **Page 73**
2. Both the number of sections and their order of appearance
   will vary from report to report.   **Page 76**

## REPORT ON SCOTSDALE-HARRISTON GAME

I. Introduction
  A. Game played at Harriston, Sat., Oct. 4
  B. Weather clear, field dry
II. Summary
  A. Scotsdale offense
    1. Strong running
    2. Weak passing
  B. Scotsdale defense
    1. Strong against running
    2. Weak against passing
III. Description
  A. Scotsdale offense
    1. Over-all ran 57 plays
    2. Running game
      a. Fullback ran 14 times for 61 yards, two TD's, long gain 23
      b. Right halfback ran 19 times for 117 yards, two TD's, long gain 36    ·
      c. Left halfback ran 16 times for 80 yards, long gain 12.
    3. Passing game—quarterback passed three times, completed one for 4 yards, had one intercepted
  B. Scotsdale defense
    1. Harriston ran 29 plays
    2. Scotsdale pass defense allowed 10 completions in 14 attempts for 146 yards
    3. Scotsdale ground defense
      a. Allowed All-League fullback 37 yards in nine carries
      b. Allowed both halfbacks 14 yards in six carries
  C. Scotsdale kicking game
    1. Kickoffs—six kickoffs for a 55-yard average
    2. Punts—four kicks for a 32-yard average
    3. PAT's—kicked three of four

*(Continued on page 62.)*

    D. Penalties
        1. Scotsdale was penalized 95 yards
        2. Harriston was penalized 35 yards
    E. Kick returns
        1. Scotsdale returned three kickoffs an average of 19 yards, long gain 37 yards
        2. Scotsdale returned six punts an average of 14 yards, long gain 29 yards
IV. Conclusions
    A. Scotsdale strong points
        1. Good running game—all backs good runners
        2. Good ball control—held ball 57 plays out of 86
        3. Good kick returns
        4. Good kickoffs, punts
        5. Good ground defense
    B. Scotsdale weak points
        1. Weak passing attack—tried only three, had one intercepted
        2. Weak passing defense—Harriston completed 10 of 14 passes, two for TD's
        3. Team tends to draw penalties
 V. Recommendations
    A. A team that is to play Scotsdale should
        1. Concentrate on a passing attack
        2. Concentrate on ground defense
VI. Appendix—Attached is a play-by-play written record of the game.

Your outline should look just about like this one. As before, we don't ask for an exact match. As long as you put the various facts into logical order, and had all six basic sections, we'll give you top marks. But if you had anything about the bands in your outline, we'll send you back to the beginning of the program! If you think you need more practice, go to page 71 and work on the business outline. If your football outline was good, go to page 66.

## REPORT ON INCREASE IN PRODUCTION COST SINCE CANCELLATION OF INCENTIVE PLAN

I. Introduction
  A. Incentive program has been in effect for 17 years.
  B. Production supervisor decided to suspend it to determine the effect on production.
  C. Suspension took effect November 1.
  D. Under incentive system, worker received $0.25 bonus for each piece over 55 produced in 8-hour shift, $0.35 for each piece over 65.
  E. Under new system, workers received $0.40 raise in hourly rate.

II. Summary
  A. Costs of producing mahogany lamp bases by shaping them on a lathe were investigated.
    1. Cost per piece under former incentive program
    2. Cost per piece under present, no-incentive program
  B. Cost per piece is 31% greater under present, no-incentive system.
  C. Workers prefer incentive system.
  D. Recommend that incentive system be reinstated.

III. Discussion
  A. Output of three workers was checked.
  B. Worker X
    1. Total time at machine was 5.7 hours on 8-hour shift.
    2. Total time at machine under incentive system was 6.5 hours
    3. Total output was 51 pieces.
    4. Total output under incentive system (checked three years ago) was 74 pieces.

*(Continued on page 64.)*

    C. Worker Y
      1. Total time at machine was 5.3 hours on 8-hour shift.
      2. Total time at machine under incentive system was 6.5 hours.
      3. Total output was 46 pieces.
      4. Total output under incentive system (checked three years ago) was 69 pieces.
    D. Worker Z
      1. Total time at machine was 5.5 hours, on 8-hour shift.
      2. Total time at machine under incentive system was 6.6 hours.
      3. Total output was 57 pieces.
      4. Total output under previous system (checked three years ago) was 84 pieces.
    E. Totalling output of X, Y, and Z, average cost per piece under incentive program was $2.47.
    F. Totalling output of X, Y, and Z, average cost per piece under present no-incentive program is $3.24.
    G. All three workers said they preferred the incentive system, since they made more money.
IV. Conclusions
    A. All three workers spent more time at their machines under the incentive system; the average time is 19 percent.
    B. All three workers produced more pieces under the incentive system; the average increase is 47 percent.
    C. Cost per piece is 31 percent greater under the no-incentive system.
 V. Recommendations
    1. The incentive system should be reinstated.
    2. The incentives paid before the system was discontinued need not be raised, at least for the present.
    3. Pay rates should be returned to former levels.

*(Continued on page 65.)*

Your outline should closely resemble the one on pages 63-64. The only tricky point was to separate the statistics correctly into discussion material and conclusion material—the percentages belong in the conclusions. And we hope you didn't include the employees' opinions on increased wages and reduced hours. We included the historical point that the incentive system dates back 17 years. Whether you did or didn't, we'll count you right.

If you feel you need more practice, try the football outline on page 70. If you don't know anything about football, it will be a real challenge. Just concentrate on breaking the facts out into categories, and you'll be all right.

If you did well on the business outline, go to the next page.

With the outline complete, the hard part of the job is done. Filling in the details takes time, but it isn't difficult. The main thing to remember is to start writing, and keep writing. Inspiration may not come immediately, but you can't sit around waiting for it. Force it. The outline gives you a subject and suggests topic sentences, so just start writing.

What you're working on now will be your first draft. You'll have to rewrite it at least once more, probably twice. You can pick up errors, inconsistencies, repetitions, and the like on the following drafts. The main thing is to get that first draft on paper. Unless your memory is photographic, you can't edit something in your head.

Write a complete first draft. Put down everything. Subsequent revisions should involve taking out excess information—you shouldn't have to scrape up additional facts to include. Don't begin writing until the facts are all on hand, and organized.

Pick out the correct statement:

1. The first draft should include the material in the major headings of the outline. The details can be filled in later.    **Page 86**
2. The sections of the report should be completed one at a time, i.e., you should polish the introduction into final form before beginning to write the discussion.    **Page 88**
3. The first draft should include all the information, and may be rough, or even sloppy, in form.    **Page 83**

*Transfer the raw notes to 3 × 5-in. cards, one fact to a card.*

You're right. Cards are about as foolproof a system as there is. (In fact, it's a good idea to take your notes on cards in the first place.) When you have one fact to a card, it's a fairly simple matter to arrange them in the correct order and to throw out the irrelevant items. The order of the outline will be determined by the format you have selected for the report. Which brings us to the question, what outline style should we use? Three are available. Which do you prefer?

**1.** The skeleton style.
  I.
    A.
      1.
        a. **Page 56**

**2.** The decimal style.
  1.
  1.1
  1.1.1
  1.1.2
  1.1.2.1
  1.1.2.1.1
  1.1.2.1.2
  1.1.2.1.3 **Page 57**

**3.** The indent style.

This one doesn't use letters or numbers at all.

You just indent a few spaces farther,

Whenever you want to go to a lower level of subordination. **Page 58**

**68**

## AIRCRAFT DISASTERS

I. Lighter-than-air craft
  A. Civilian
    1. In February, 1922, the dirigible Roma crashed off Hampton Roads, Va.
    2. In April, 1933, the dirigible Akron crashed off the New Jersey coast.
    3. In February, 1935, the dirigible Macon crashed off Point Sur, Calif.
  B. Military
    1. In July, 1960, the U.S. Navy blimp ZPG-3W crashed off the New Jersey coast.
II. Heavier-than-air craft
  A. Civilian
    1. In October, 1947, a United Air Lines plane crashed at Bryce Canyon, Utah.
    2. In February, 1952, a National Airlines DC-6 crashed at Elizabeth, N.J.
    3. In April, 1958, a Capital Airlines Viscount crashed at Midland, Mich.
    4. In September, 1961, a TWA Constellation crashed at Hinsdale, Ill.
  B. Military
    1. In July, 1945, a U.S. Army B-25 crashed into the Empire State Building in New York City.
    2. In March, 1951, a USAF C-124 crashed in the Atlantic Ocean.
    3. In December, 1952, a USAF C-124 crashed at Moses Lake, Wash.
    4. In June, 1953, a USAF C-124 crashed near Tokyo, Japan.
    5. In December, 1960, a USAF C-131 crashed in Munich, Germany.

*(Continued on page 69.)*

Your outline should look pretty much like the one on page 68. Note that it is a combination of a topical outline and a chronological outline—items are listed chronologically within types. It would also be correct if you used roman numerals for "Civilian" and "Military," then broke these down into lighter-than-air and heavier-than-air craft. You might have gone a step further and classified the crashes by where they occurred, in the U.S. or outside it. We'll give you extra points if you went that far. We'll count you wrong only if your outline used for major headings something other than "Civilian," "Military," "Lighter-than-air craft," or "Heavier-than-air craft," or if you didn't list the crashes in chronological order.

Now let's see how you do on a real report outline. You can have a choice. If you're a sports fan (specifically football), go to page 70 and outline a football scouting report. If you'd rather work on a business subject, go to page 71 and outline a report on a cost analysis based on time and motion study. Best of all, do them both.

You'd rather work on a football report. All right, arrange the facts in the following paragraph into an outline for a report to be organized by topics, and having all six of the standard report sections.

On Saturday, October 4, George Wilson, Assistant Line Coach for the Midville High School football team, scouted the performance of the Scotsdale team in its game with Harriston. Midville will play Scotsdale on October 11. Scotsdale won the game 27-13. During the game, Scotsdale ran 57 plays, Harriston, 29. Scotsdale threw three passes, completing one for a 4-yard gain. One pass was intercepted. Harriston threw 14 passes, completing 10 for a total of 146 yards. None was intercepted. Both Harriston's touchdowns were scored on pass plays, one of 24 and one of 46 yards. Scotsdale's fullback carried the ball 14 times for 61 yards and two touchdowns; his long gain was 23 yards. The right halfback carried the ball 19 times for 117 yards and one touchdown; his long gain was 36 yards. The left halfback carried the ball 16 times for 80 yards, with a long gain of 12 yards. Scotsdale punted four times for a 32-yard average. At halftime both bands performed well, with the Scotsdale band having an edge in intricacy of formations, while the Harriston band maintained straighter lines. Harriston's All-League fullback was held to 37 yards gained in nine carries. Harriston's two halfbacks gained 14 yards on six carries between them. The field was dry, the weather clear.

The game was played at the Harriston Field. Coach Wilson decided that in preparing for the Scotsdale game, Midville should concentrate on a passing offense, and prepare the defense to meet a running attack. Scotsdale was penalized 95 yards, Harriston 35. Coach Wilson included a play-by-play record of the game with his report. Scotsdale's kickoff specialist averaged 55 yards on 5 kickoffs. Scotsdale kicked 3 of 4 extra points, Harriston 1 of 2. Scotsdale returned three kickoffs an average of 19 yards, long gain 37 yards, and returned six punts an average of 14 yards, long gain 29 yards.

When you have completed your outline compare it with the one on pages 61-62.

You would prefer to prepare your report outline on a business subject. Fine. Here are the facts. Throw out the unnecessary ones, and construct a report outline containing the first five basic sections. (You won't need an appendix.)

Early last fall, the Production Supervisor of the Landry Lamp Works decided to test the economy of the incentive production system. This system, which the company had used for 17 years, provided an incentive bonus for each piece above a predetermined number produced by each worker. The specific items checked were mahogany lamp bases, which are turned on lathes and shaped by hand. The three men who produce these lamp bases were formerly paid a bonus of $0.25 for each piece in excess of 55 they turned out during an 8-hour shift, and a bonus of $0.35 for each piece in excess of 65. Effective November 1, they were given a pay increase of $0.40 per hour, and the incentive bonuses were discontinued. In February of the following year, Junior Engineer George Millar was asked to check production under the no-incentive plan, establish a comparison of costs for the two plans, and recommend whether the no-incentive plan should be continued. Millar checked the output of the three workers. He found that worker X was at his machine for 5.7 hours during the 8-hour shift, and produced 51 pieces; worker Y was at his machine for 5.3 hours of the 8-hour shift, and produced 46 pieces; worker Z was at his machine 5.5 hours of the 8-hour shift, and produced 57 pieces. Millar then checked these performance figures against the results of a similar check run three years before, when the incentive system was in effect. At that time, worker X had stayed at his machine 6.5 hours during the 8-hour shift, and produced 74 pieces; worker Y had been at his machine 6.5 hours, and produced 69 pieces, worker Z had been at his machine 6.6 hours, and produced 84 pieces. Millar interviewed all three workes, and they all said that they preferred the incentive system. They also said that a general pay raise and a shorter work week would be well received by the plant's employees. Millar then figured out the cost per piece for the lamp bases produced by each system. He found that under the

*(Continued on page 72.)*

incentive system, the cost per piece was $2.47; under the no-incentive system, the cost per piece was $3.24. The cost per piece is 31 percent greater under the no-incentive system. All three workers spent more time at their machines when working under the incentive system; the average difference was 19 percent. All three workers produced more pieces when working under the incentive system; the average difference was 47 percent. Millar decided that the use of the incentive system meant a definite and considerable saving to the company, and felt that it should once again be put into effect. Because of the eagerness of the workers to return to the incentive system, Millar felt that there was no need to increase the incentive bonuses, at least for the present.

Prepare your outline, then go to page 63 and compare it with ours.

*All reports will have all six basic sections, and in the same order.*

No, you're wrong. As we said in Chapter 2, not all reports need all these sections. Even if all six are needed, the audience may require that you arrange them in an unusual order. There are very few hard-and-fast rules in report writing.

Go back to page 60 and make another selection.

*Write the first draft of the report.*

A thousand times, no! Please pay closer attention. We just said that "the first writing you do will be the preparation of an outline." If you skip the outline, you'll have to go through several extra drafts before you get your data into the proper sequence, taking several steps to do the work of one: an outline.

Go back to page 55 and make another selection.

*Outline 1.*

Not quite. This one is all right except for the body. Here you've used the very general headings, "Discussion" and "Details." Don't you think that headings more suited to the experimental work being done would be better?

Go back to page 77 and make another selection.

*Both the number of sections and their order of appearance will vary from report to report.*

Of course they will. Depending on audience, any feature of a report can be modified. You may think that the titles we've given the six sections are too general (or maybe you object to titling a part of your report "Body"). Here is a list of more descriptive headings that can be used instead. You may want to use more than one heading in a section—for instance, "Tests to be Made" and "Apparatus Used" are both introductory topics.

*For Introduction*

1. Statement of the Problem
2. Subject
3. Preface
4. Objectives
5. Foreword
6. Purpose of the Report
7. Parts (or Materials) Tested
8. Apparatus Used
9. Definition of Terms
10. Tests to be Made

*For Summary*

1. Abstract
2. Synopsis

*For Body*

1. Discussion
2. Details
3. Experiment (or Investigation) Procedure
4. Records of Tests (Experiments)
5. Description
6. Data Obtained

*For Conclusions*

1. Results
2. Interpretation of Data
3. Results and Conclusions

*For Recommendations*

1. Proposed Solution to Problem
2. Suggestions
3. Comments
4. Opinions

*For Appendixes*

1. Charts and Graphs
2. Illustrations
3. Computations
4. Exhibits
5. Tables

*(Continued on page 77.)*

As you can see, some of these headings have virtually the same meaning—for example, Foreword and Preface, Suggestions and Recommendations. They are included just to give you the chance to add a little variety.

From the list below, select the headings you would use in a report on the testing and evaluation of the performance of a forklift truck that has been suggested for purchase. Assume that your audience wants a report in the standard topical format.

**1.**  I. Introduction
       II. Summary
      III. Discussion
           A. Details
           B. Description
       IV. Conclusions
        V. Recommendations
       VI. Appendix 1—Tables of Performance          **Page 75**

**2.**  I. Introduction
           A. Parts Tested
           B. Apparatus
       II. Summary
      III. Body
           A. Experiment Procedure
           B. Records of Tests and Experiments
       IV. Conclusions
           A. Interpretation of Data
           B. Results and Conclusions
        V. Recommendations
       VI. Appendix—Data Tables                      **Page 85**

**3.**  I. Introduction—Statement of the problem
       II. Summary
      III. Body
           A. Discussion
           B. Description of problem situation
       IV. Conclusions
        V. Recommendations—Proposed solution of problem
                                                     **Page 78**

**78**

*Outline 3.*

No, we're afraid not. All the headings in this outline are very general, not at all suited to the scientific report you're outlining. Since we're describing a scientific test, we should use headings that are worded accordingly.

Go back to page 77 and try again.

*Summary 2.*

Very good. This summary gives a brief statement of test results, and recommends appropriate action. A reader who could not spare the time to read the entire report could become familiar with the basic facts in about 30 seconds, and that's exactly the function of a summary.

The next part you'll be writing is the body, which is the biggest, and about which we can say the least. All you do is put down the facts, according to your outline. There just are no hard-and-fast rules about writing the body—its content is totally dependent on subject and audience, and its structure was determined when you wrote the outline. So writing the first draft of the body boils down to putting meat on the bones of your outline, as completely as you can.

When the body is complete, you can heave a sigh of relief and begin tying the loose ends together—drawing conclusions and making recommmendations (only, of course, if your audience wants you to include these steps). These sections, too, will be written directly from your outline. There are a couple of points to keep in mind about each.

Go to page 99.

**Outline 1.**

SIZE AND TEMPERATURE OF VARIOUS PLANETS
IN THE SOLAR SYSTEM

I. Mercury
   A. Size
      1. Smallest planet in the solar system
      2. Diameter 3100 miles
   B. Temperature
      1. On light side: 750°F
      2. On dark side: almost absolute zero (−459°F)
II. Venus
   A. Size
      1. Virtually the same size as Earth
      2. Diameter 7800 miles
   B. Temperature
      1. On light side: about 212°F
      2. On dark side: about −10°F
III. Mars
   A. Size
      1. A little more than one-half the size of Earth
      2. Diameter 4220 miles
   B. Temperature
      1. On light side: 50 to 70°F
      2. On dark side: −90 to −100°F          **Page 91**

**Outline 2.**

## SIZE AND TEMPERATURE OF VARIOUS PLANETS IN THE SOLAR SYSTEM

I. Size
  A. Mercury
    1. Smallest planet in the solar system
    2. Diameter 3100 miles
  B. Venus
    1. Virtually the same size as Earth
    2. Diameter 7800 miles
  C. Mars
    1. Little more than one-half the size of Earth
    2. Diameter 4220 miles
II. Temperature
  A. Mercury
    1. On light side: 750°F
    2. On dark side: almost absolute zero (−459°F)
  B. Venus
    1. On light side: about 212°F
    2. On dark side: about −10°F
  C. Mars
    1. On light side: from 50 to 70°F
    2. On dark side: from −90 to −100°F **Page 87**

**82**

**Outline 3.**

SIZE AND TEMPERATURE OF VARIOUS PLANETS
IN THE SOLAR SYSTEM

I. Mercury
  A. Size
    1. Smallest planet in the solar system
    2. Diameter 3100 miles
  B. Temperature
    1. On light side: 750°F
    2. On dark side: almost absolute zero (−459°F)
    3. Mercury has no atmosphere
    4. Mercury has no seasons
II. Venus
  A. Size
    1. Venus is called the sister planet of Earth
    2. Virtually the same size as Earth
    3. Diameter 7800 miles
  B. Temperature
    1. On light side: about 212°F
    2. On dark side: about −10°F
III. Mars
  A. Size
    1. A little more than half as big as Earth
    2. One year on Mars is equal to about two years on Earth
    3. Diameter 4220 miles
  B. Temperature
    1. On light side: from 50 to 70°F
    2. On dark side: from −90 to −100°F    **Page 89**

*The first draft should include all the information, and may be rough, or even sloppy, in form.*

Right. Just so all the facts are present, you're in good shape. It shouldn't, of course, be so sloppy that you can't read it, but a certain amount of sloppiness won't do any harm. At the worst, you'll have to go through an extra draft.

The first part of your report that you will put on paper will be the introduction.

Go to page 97.

Which of the following fulfills the requirements of a good summary?

1. After conducting a thorough investigation of the properties and performance of three models offered by competing companies, I recommend that the Finley Model A Water Cooler be purchased for installation in the lobby.     **Page 90**

2. The Finley Model A Water Cooler was tested against two competitive models, and proved superior in the following ways: larger capacity by 21 percent than either of the other two models; lower operating cost by 6 percent than its nearest competitor; more attractive appearance, as determined by a survey of 50 office workers asked to express an opinion; and price, which is 8 percent lower than its nearest competitor. By reason of these four areas of superiority, it is recommended for purchase and installation in the lobby.     **Page 79**

3. At the Board of Directors meeting last month, it was decided that a water cooler should be installed in the lobby of the corporation offices at 16682 Front Street. Last week, tests of three competitive models were completed. The three models tested were the Finley Model A, the Hackworth 61-A6, and the Butterbread Super DeLuxe.

### COMPARISON

| Name | Price | Capacity (gallons) | Votes gained | Operating Cost (per month) |
|------|-------|--------------------|--------------|----------------------------|
| Hackworth | $116.84 | 2 | 13 | $4.20 |
| Butterbread | 131.98 | 1.8 | 18 | 5.16 |
| Finley | 107.49 | 2.53 | 19 | 3.95 |

**Page 93**

*Outline 2.*

Right you are. These headings cover all the kinds of things you're going to have to say in a report on an experiment.

How would you outline the following facts, to fit the title "Size and Temperature of Various Planets in the Solar System"? (Discard irrelevant facts.)

Mercury is the smallest planet in the solar system.
The nighttime temperature on Venus is about $-10°$F.
Mercury has no atmosphere.
The diameter of Mars is 4220 miles.
The daytime temperature on Mars is 50 to 70°F.
The temperature on the dark side of Mercury is almost absolute zero ($-459°$F).
The diameter of Venus is 200 miles less than the diameter of Earth.
Venus is called the "sister planet" of Earth.
On Mars, the temperature at midnight is $-90$ to $-100°$F.
The diameter of Mercury is 3100 miles.
On Venus, the temperature on the light side is about 212°F.
Mercury's diameter is less than half that of Earth.
One year on Mars equals about two years on Earth.
The temperature on the light side of Mercury is 750°F.
Mercury has no seasons.
Mars is a little more than half as big as Earth.

Prepare your outline, then compare it with Outlines 1, 2, and 3 on pages 80-82. The wording need not be exactly similar; choose the one that matches yours most closely in order of presentation.

*The first draft should include the material in the major headings of the outline. The details can be filled in later.*

Now, where did you get that idea? Quite the opposite is true. Every available detail should be included. In preparing your outline you will have already cast out whatever material is obviously unnecessary. Everything that appears in the outline should be in the first draft. If some of the information should turn out to be unnecessary, you can eliminate it in the next draft.

Go back to page 66 and select another answer.

*Outline 2.*

This is one of the ways to do it. You discarded the irrelevant facts and came up with a good outline. It might be a little better to break the data down by planets, as was done in Outline 1, but this isn't a vital point.

Go to page 91, the answer page for Outline 1.

**88**

*The sections of the report should be written one at a time; i.e., you should polish the introduction into final form before beginning to write the discussion.*

No, this is not the best way to operate. The reason is that changes in one section may affect what you have said in a previous section. It's annoying to have to go back and rewrite a supposedly "finished" section because of a minor change in a later one.

Go back to page 66 and make another selection.

*Outline 3.*

Well, the outline *form* is all right, but you've thrown in a few unnecessary items. For instance, are the facts that Mercury has no atmosphere and no seasons important in a discussion of size and temperature? The same criticism applies to the fact that Venus is called the sister planet of Earth, or that one year on Mars is equal to two years on Earth. In any outline (and, of course, in any report) stick to the relevant facts.

Go back to pages 80-82 and make another selection.

*Summary 1.*

Well, that's certainly a brief summary, all right. But there isn't enough to it. We said that the summary should state the reasons for your conclusions and recommendations. This one fails to satisfy that condition.

Go back to page 84 and make another selection.

*Outline 1.*

Very good. Your outline classifies the data by planets, and presents it in good order, with no unnecessary facts. Now let's try another. This time, select the best kind of outline to use, and organize the facts accordingly.

## AIRCRAFT DISASTERS

In June, 1953, a U.S. Air Force C-124 crashed near Tokyo, Japan.

In October, 1947, a United Air Lines plane crashed at Bryce Canyon, Utah.

In April, 1958, a Capital Airlines Viscount crashed at Midland, Mich.

In February, 1922, the U.S. dirigible Roma crashed at Hampton Rds., Va.

In December, 1960, a USAF C-131 crashed in Munich, Germany.

In December, 1952, a USAF C-124 crashed at Moses Lake, Wash.

In April, 1933, the dirigible Akron crashed off the New Jersey coast.

In February, 1952, a National Airlines DC-6 crashed in Elizabeth, N.J.

In September, 1961, a TWA Constellation crashed at Hinsdale, Ill.

In February, 1935, the dirigible Macon crashed off Point Sur, Calif.

In March, 1951, a USAF C-124 crashed in the Atlantic Ocean.

In July, 1945, a U.S. Army B-25 crashed into the Empire State Building, New York City.

In July, 1960, U.S. Navy blimp ZPG-3W crashed off the New Jersey coast.

Here's a hint: dirigibles can be called lighter-than-air craft; airplanes, heavier-than-air craft.

Make up your outline, then turn to page 68.

*Justification, method, and definition are covered well, purpose and scope poorly.*

Right! You have a good idea of what a good introduction should contain.

The second part of the report is the summary. As you remember from Chapter 2, this section gives the gist of the report without going into detail. As a rule of thumb, assume that the summary will take up about 5 percent of your report. You should be able to summarize a 10-page report in about half a page. The summary should contain the most important things you have to say—your main conclusions and recommendations, as well as the facts on which you based them. Working directly from your outline, you should be able to come up with a good summary quite easily.

Go to page 84.

*Summary 3.*

We think not. Not only does this so-called summary present a table that rightly belongs in the body of the report, but it never does make any recommendation. This is the worst kind of summary.

Go back to page 84 and make another selection.

*Purpose, scope, and method are covered well, definition and justification poorly.*

Do you really think so? We agree that method is well covered, but what do you really know about the purpose and the scope of the report? The only limiting factor you're sure of is the $1,500 budget. Aren't these sentences considerably more informative?

*Purpose:* The purpose of the report is to uncover the causes of the decline in walk-in trade, as well as ways in which the decline can be stopped.

*Scope:* Conclusions in the area of customer motivation were drawn strictly on the basis of information obtained in the interviews conducted outside the main entrance. Changes in economic conditions in the region over the past three years are thought to be a negligible factor, and have not been taken into account.

Also, look again and see if you don't agree that justification was provded, and at least one term ("walk-in trade") was defined.

Go back to page 98 and make another selection.

*You recommend that the town install parking meters.*

We don't feel very optimistic about your future in politics. Your report said that 70 percent of the townspeople interviewed were opposed to the meters. Even though you're a new man, you must be aware that the mayor and councilmen are responsive to public opinion. Your choice, though honest, has the fault of being unrealistic.

Read page 105 again, and make another choice.

*Method and scope are covered well, purpose, justification, and definition poorly.*

You are about half right. We agree that method is covered well, but where do we learn anything about scope? And it's true that all we can do in the area of purpose is make assumptions. But the first two sentences are devoted to justification and the last sentence defines a term. (If you're not sure what we mean by justification, scope, and the rest, review them on page 97.)

Go back to page 98 and make another selection.

The introduction will, logically enough, vary in size with the length of the report. It provides whatever background the audience needs to prepare him to dig into the body. Informal, horizontally directed reports often require only the briefest of introductions, or none at all. Longer reports require more.

Here are the types of introductory material that should be supplied with a typical semiformal or formal report five or more pages long:

1. *Scope:* Define what the report covers, and, often equally important, what it does not cover. Make clear any assumptions which were made that might have affected the conclusions. If there is pertinent evidence that you were unable to analyze for reasons of time, money, etc., make the audience aware of it.

2. *Purpose:* You defined the purpose of the report in your own mind when you were thinking about the audience. However, you must supply to your reader, particularly for the secondary audience, a statement of what your report is intended to accomplish.

3. *Method:* How was the information in the report collected? By research, investigation, testing, or experimentation? Explain the procedures that were used.

4. *Justification:* Particularly in longer reports, which may involve a couple of hundred dollars' worth of your time, you may be asked to include a statement of why the report is necessary, and who authorized it.

5. *Definition of terms:* This consideration is particularly dependent on audience. The bigger your secondary audience, the more you will have to think about defining terms that have a particular meaning in the context of your report.

*(Continued on page 98.)*

As with so many other parts of a report, the introduction may contain any or all of these items, in whatever order suits the situation. They may be written up in outline form, or combined in a single paragraph. It is important for you to know all five, though, just in case they are needed.

In the following introduction, which of the five parts are covered well, and which poorly?

Over the past three years, walk-in trade at Bloomingsak's Department Store has decreased considerably. Therefore, Vice-president Ed Butler authorized $1,500 to be spent on a detailed investigation of the situation, the fruition of which is this report.

The problem was approached in two ways: (1) A survey, conducted by the interview method, of 500 passers-by in the immediate area of the main entrance and (2) a study of changes in traffic patterns in the four-block-square area surrounding Bloomingsak's (in which study the files of the City Traffic Department were made available). For the purposes of this report, "walk-in trade" is defined as including customers who happened to be passing by, as opposed to those who left home with the specific intention of shopping at Bloomingsak's.

1. Purpose, scope and method are covered well, definition and justification poorly.   **Page 94**
2. Justification, method, and definition are covered well, purpose and scope poorly.   **Page 92**
3. Method and scope are covered well, purpose, justification, and definition poorly.   **Page 96**

The conclusions are the crux of the whole report—the reason you wrote it in the first place. They may be obvious to anyone, or they may result from careful weighing of conflicting bits of evidence, but *they must derive logically and clearly from your data.* If the evidence doesn't prove anything, there's no use handing in a report. Present your conclusions and support them with references to the body of the report, or to material in an appendix These references need not repeat large quantities of material in these sections, but merely should indicate the page on which the supporting data will be found. Actually, the more tersely you can state your conclusions, the greater weight they will carry.

*(Continued on page 100.)*

Which of the following is a good set of conclusions?

1. The town of Pottsville should purchase 200 parking meters at $26.50 each, since the "pro" factors outweigh the "con" factors, as detailed in the body of this report.          **Page 108**

2. The inquiry into the feasibility of purchasing parking meters for the main street of Pottsville produced the following results:

Factors in favor of the parking meters:

A. The cost of procuring land for off-street lots, and of the construction of these lots, would be 19 times as great as the cost of purchasing and installing meters.

B. Studies were conducted in the two towns in the USA most similar to Pottsville in population, economic conditions, and other pertinent factors, (selection made by IBM 7090 computer), namely, Big Toe, Tennessee, and Frozen Dog, Wyoming. In both towns, business in main street stores increased 23 percent after parking meters were installed (See page 17 for details.)

Factors opposing parking meters:

A. A survey of 853 residents showed that 601 were opposed to the idea of installing parking meters.

Taking into account all of these considerations, it is recommended that Pottsville proceed with the purchase of 200 meters at $26.50 each.          **Page 103**

3. Conclusions:

a. Seventy percent of a random sample of Pottsville residents opposed parking meters. (See page 3.)

b. The installation of parking meters caused business in main street stores to increase by 23 percent in two towns that were studied because of their close similarity to Pottsville. (See page 7.)

c. The cost of buying land and building off-street parking lots would be 19 times as great as the cost of buying and installing 200 parking meters. (See page 11.)          **Page 105**

*You recommend that no action be taken pending further study of public reaction.*

Very good. This is the only reasonable course. Your report demonstrates forcibly that parking meters would be good for the town. Thus the indicated procedure would be to try to convince the public—maybe you'll get the assignment of writing a report on the possible ways to accomplish that. Your report did its job, but you can't expect too much of it. You'll only create problems for yourself if you do.

Go to page 102.

**102**

**102**

Having completed the first draft, you have a big decision to make: Is the first draft so sloppy that a typist couldn't possibly read it, or could she? If it's sloppy, you're stuck with the job of writing out a second, legible handwritten copy. Either way, sooner or later you will have a typewritten draft, which should go through two stages of criticism.

First, you yourself should review it as carefully as you can. Look for errors in spelling, sentence structure, etc., as well as in clarity and logicality of presentation. You will be surprised at how few you pick up—by now you're so familiar with the material that everything looks right. Next, have a friend or associate review it. This is a very important step, particularly if it's essential that you create a favorable impression on your audience. It's very probable that a new pair of eyes will pick out some points that need clearing up. (This is no reflection on you as a report writer. All authors recognize the fact that someone who hasn't seen the work before finds it easier to spot mistakes.)

Which of the following statements is true?

1. After the author has reviewed his own report, he should let someone else check it over.    **Page 109**
2. The author should have let someone else review the typewritten draft, then look it over himself.    **Page 107**

*Set 2.*

No. This is an incorrect choice for two reasons:

1. It's too wordy. The fact that two towns studied were selected by IBM 7090 computer, the names of the towns—are these facts vital to the report? No.

2. There's a recommendation tacked onto the end. Conclusions deal only with the past. Recommendations for future action belong in a separate section.

Go back to page 100 and make another selection.

*You recommend that Pottsville not install parking meters.*

Why? Your report states that two towns very similar to Pottsville both benefited economically from parking meters. Perhaps the public in those towns were opposed at first, too, but came around after an educational campaign. Also, it stands to reason that at least a couple of the Pottsville councilmen are local merchants, who would be tempted by that 23 percent rise in profits. You aren't making yourself popular with them. Remember, your interpretation of the conclusions is not necessarily everybody's.

Reread page 105 and make another choice.

*Set 3.*

Right. These conclusions are stated briefly, and they don't get into the area of recommendations. If your audience has specified that your report contain recommendations, these will follow immediately after the conclusions. The important thing to remember about recommendations is this: Just as conclusions derive from the body of the report, recommendations derive from conclusions. *Be very sure that you don't get carried away and make recommendations that are unrealistic.* A little caution will go a long way at this stage, especially if there is any appreciable amount of conflicting evidence. Conclusions can be interpreted differently by different people, so unless the position you recommend is easily defensible, don't be too persistent about it. Once again, knowledge of your audience (or lack of it) will guide you in how far to go.

Let's consider again the Pottsville parking meter affair. Assume that you are the second newest member of the town council, and that your immediate audience is the mayor, your secondary audience the town council.

Which is the most reasonable approach?

1. You recommend that the town install parking meters.
**Page 95**
2. You recommend that no action be taken pending further study of public reaction.   **Page 101**
3. You recommend that Pottsville not install parking meters.
**Page 104**
4. You recommend that Pottsville build off-street parking lots.
**Page 106**

*You recommend that Pottsville build off-street parking lots.*

You're really out in left field this time. Your report dealt with parking *meters*. The only thing you know about parking *lots* is that the bill would be 19 times as big. Do you think that's a good basis for making such a recommendation?

Reread page 105 and make another selection.

*The author should let someone else review the typewritten draft, then look it over himself.*

We think we caught you not paying enough attention. Reread page 102 and make the correct selection.

*Set 1.*

No, you're wrong. This isn't a conclusion at all, it's a recommendation. Conclusions just give the results of your research; they *do not* make any statements about what should be done in the future.

Go back to page 100 and make another selection.

*After the author has reviewed his own report, he should let someone else check it over.*

Correct. And when the final check is finished, and any necessary changes have been made, the report can be typed in final form, addressed, and sent on its way.

This ends the chapter on the mechanics of report writing. Turn now to page 113, the first page of Chapter 4, which deals with report language and style.

# 4

# Report Language
# and Style

Here are two paragraphs of description:

1. Easterly, atop the primordial pines, the inception of en
ing day makes nacreous the pristine brilliance of Queen Venus,
then bedims, one at a time, the glimmering members of her reti-
nue. In the brightening crepuscule, the burning orb that hovers
just below the rim of earth sends aloft faint fingers of lambent
luminosity, and lights the east with a pavonine spectrum of
shades—a parti-colored panorama of bruise, azure, topaz, ochre,
rose. The sun ascends; the delicate hints of color give way to a
florid pageantry of resplendently pure hues which, leaping to the
zenith, drives cowering night to the western horizon, and away.

2. The night was moonless. The hill on the far side of the lake
was shapeless and indistinct against the black sky. The sky began
to lighten, and the stars grew dim. The stand of blue spruce on
the hill became visible in the surface of the lake. Now you could
see a deer trail at the edge of the woods, and from the trail a doe
came down to drink.

What can you tell about the author(s) of these two passages?

1. Both passages were written by the same person.     **Page 114**
2. The passages were written by different persons.     **Page 122**

1. Both passages were written by the same person.     **Page 114**
2. The passages were written by different persons.     **Page 122**

*Both passages were written by the same person.*

No, you're wrong. What is there about these paragraphs that makes you think they had the same author? Do they both use the same kinds of words (simple or obscure)? Do they have similar sentence structure? Go back to page 113. Read them again with these questions in mind, then follow the directions for the other answer.

*Paragraph 2.*

This is a much better paragraph than the first one. It's better because it's shorter, and it contains about twice as many specific facts. But we would like to make a couple of comments about the style.

This is what we call the formal style. There are no personal words (*we, he, us,* etc.), no contractions, no colloquialisms or slang. It is written in the third person—("Mr. Harris decided")—and in the passive voice—("the contract was awarded")—This style is perfectly good, and widely used. But it is not lively or interesting, and gets dull when read in long stretches. Later on in this chapter, you'll learn to avoid the passive voice.

You may object that slang, contractions, and colloquialisms aren't good writing by the standards of our schools. Quite right. But conversation, the best form of communication, doesn't observe all the rules we learned in school. The purpose of a report is communication. Communication is best achieved in relaxed circumstances. Therefore, an easy-reading, conversational report will make your audience more receptive, and he will retain more of what he reads. This pronouncement has to be qualified (there are no absolutes in report writing): If your immediate audience prefers a stilted, formal style, and detests slang, of course you would write to suit him.

Go back to page 120 and select the correct answer.

*Paragraph 3.*

Very good. That's our favorite, too. It presents the facts just as well as Paragraph 2 does, and it presents them in a pleasant, conversational style. It's our feeling that we communicate best when we communicate informally. The casual approach gets us closer to the audience and makes him more receptive to what we have to say. Unless your audience is the sort that demands the formal approach, your report will be better for being a little lively. But, as with everything else in your report, the audience is the final authority. You wouldn't write a casual report to a grouch. Neither would you write formally to a good friend. If there's any doubt, lean to the side of formality. An audience that would only be bored by too much formality may well be offended if you're overly casual.

The one style that you should *never* allow to creep into your work is the ornate. We define the formal style as the use of impersonal words and the strict avoidance of contractions, colloquialisms, and slang. The ornate adds to this list the unnecessary use of long words and involved sentences, usually with the intention of impressing the reader. A good many of the reports you come across will be in more or less ornate style. Paragraph 1 on page 120 is an example.

Where did the ornate style come from, and why is it so widely used? Most of us have been exposed to the ornate style since childhood, in court, in church, and in political oratory (although there's a trend toward simplicity among the current generation of politicians). We're talking now about three different ornate styles, of course, but they have in common the fact that a respected individual is talking in an imposing manner on a subject about which the audience is not fully informed. The talker is well dressed, perhaps in some distinctive costume. He is an expert public speaker. In a word, he's impressive.

*(Continued on page 117.)*

The natural result is that the average person grows up with a built-in respect for the ornate style, probably without ever having a conscious thought on the subject. And when a situation arises—a speech, a business letter, a report—in which he wants to make a favorable impression while communicating, he tends to assemble whatever fragments of various ornate styles are kicking around in his mind.

This is a mistake, for the simple reason that ornate styles are more impressive than they are communicative. The typical user of an ornate style wants not just to convey information, but to shape people's thoughts as well. Only another expert in the field can communicate effectively with the ornate stylist. This is quite contrary to the purpose of a report, which is to communicate briefly and understandably.

Clarity and brevity are simply not compatible with the ornate style, and for this reason you should avoid it entirely. Formality is permissible in most cases, and required in some. It is not as good for general report usage as the casual, which helps get you on friendly terms with your audience.

Look at this sentence in the casual style:

It looks like the fat's in the fire. As far as Beamish can tell, there isn't a chance in the world that we can meet the delivery schedule.

When would you use it?

1. In a report to a fellow supervisor, "putting him on board" with regard to a scheduling problem.   **Page 124**
2. In a report to a company vice-president, whom you do not know personally.   **Page 121**
3. In a report to be circulated among various department heads. **Page 123**

*Paragraph 1.*

Do you really like that one? It's a gold mine of bad usage. Let's look at it again.

As a result of a *persistent and continuing* undersupply of component J-7 (the inside rotor balance wheel) *it was determined* by *cognizant authority* that additional *and/or* new suppliers of the *aforementioned* component should be approached *with a view to increasing the number that would be kept on hand in the parts storage depot.* After receiving bids and comparing samples of work submitted, *it was decided* that the contract for component J-7 would be terminated at the end of its current period of application, and a new award made, this time to the Ace Metal Products Co. of Denver.

This paragraph is an example of the *ornate style.* It is:

1. repetitive ("persistent and continuing"),
2. fuzzy ("cognizant authority"),
3. wordy ("with a view to increasing," "kept on hand in the parts storage depot"),
4. dull ("it was decided," "it was determined"),
5. selfconscious about words ("aforementioned," "and/or").

The writer wants to communicate, but he also wants to impress the reader with his vocabulary and style. He adopts a sort of semilegal tone ("aforementioned"). His long, involved sentences are impressive in a way, but hard to read. In short, his style is just the opposite of what a report style should be—to-the-point, factual, and easy to read.

Go back to page 120 and make another selection.

*You're playing games—there's nothing wrong with those words.*

No, we're not playing games. You've probably seen some of these forms before, but that doesn't make them correct.

Go back to page 126 and make another selection.

Everyone has a style, even you. Yours may not be particularly distinctive, but the words you use, and the way you put them together, give you a style that is at least slightly different from any other. The question is, how does your style stack up against good report-writing style? More basically, what is good report-writing style?

We can best teach style by showing you examples of bad style and telling you how to improve them. Which of the following paragraphs would you say is written in a good report-writing style?

1. As a result of a persistent and continuing undersupply of component J-7 (the inside rotor balance wheel) it was determined by cognizant authority that additional and/or new suppliers of the aforementioned component should be approached with a view to increasing the number that would be kept on hand in the parts storage depot. After receiving bids and comparing samples of work submitted, it was decided that the contract for component J-7 would be terminated at the end of its current period of application, and a new award made, this time to the Ace Metal Products Co. of Denver.     **Page 118**

2. During the past six months, it has been necessary to shut down the production line on four occasions for a total of ten hours, because of a shortage of component J-7, the inside rotor balance wheel. Frank Harris, Inventory Control Manager, decided that the company should find a new supplier of this part. Bids were invited, and samples requested. Testing and evaluation indicated that the Ace Metal Products Co. of Denver had submitted the best part. Since AMP was also the low bidder, it was awarded the contract, effective January 1st of next year.     **Page 115**

3. To bring you up to date on the J-7 component problem: As you probably know, we lost 10 hours of production time during the past six months because the supplier wasn't meeting delivery dates. Frank Harris in Inventory Control decided to find a new supplier. We're going to give the new contract to Ace Metal Products Co. of Denver, for two reasons: Testing and evaluation showed that the AMP sample had a reliability on the order of 92 percent, and its price was 2 percent below the next lower bidder's.     **Page 116**

FROM PAGE 117                                        **121**

*In a report to a company vice-president, whom you do not know personally.*

Well, happy job hunting. That casual approach will land you out in the street. You're reporting a serious problem, one that could cost your company a pile of money in penalties, not to mention future business. To put the problem in these terms to a vice-president is almost suicidal, especially if you don't even know the man! Remember, we said to make any errors on the side of formality.
Wouldn't this be better?

The scheduled completion date on the Foley job was the first of the month. The Plant Supervisor, Henry Beamish, reports that this date cannot be met.

This style is much more formal, but still retains a couple of personal words to give the casual touch.

Go back to 117 and make another choice.

*The passages were written by different persons.*

Right. Even without knowing the sources of the material, you could see that two different minds were at work. Each style of writing is so distinctive that you recognized that one man could not have been responsible for both.

Go to page 120.

*In a report to be circulated among various department heads.*

No, you're being too casual in this case. Maybe some of the department heads will accept your casual attitude toward a fairly serious problem, but it's a cinch that not all of them will.

Here's a possible way to improve it:

The scheduled completion date on the Foley job was the first of the month. The Plant Supervisor, Henry Beamish, reports that this date cannot be met.

This is, of course, formal style. But it hardly seems out of place when you're discussing a serious problem. Remember, you can do a lot less damage by being too formal than by being too casual.

Go back to page 117 and make another selection.

*In a report to a fellow supervisor, "putting him on board" with re-
gard to a scheduling problem.*

Right, this is the only one of these situations in which you could
possibly use that approach. You're talking about a serious problem
here, and someone who wasn't a good friend of yours would very
likely regard your style as unnecessarily flippant. A better way to
say it (and still use the casual style) would be:

> We've run into a serious problem on the Foley job. According to
> Beamish, we simply can't meet that first of the month delivery
> date.

A "good" casual style would be along the lines of these examples:

Instead of:
> As an examination of the accompanying charts will demonstrate,
> the metal on the leading edge of the wing will be heated to the
> melting point when the aircraft has attained a speed of 1500 mph.

We could say:
> As you can see from the charts, the leading edge of the wing will
> melt at 1500 mph.

Instead of:
> Prospects seem good that, barring unforeseen developments, the
> delivery schedule will be met.

We could use:
> We're quite confident that we can meet the delivery schedule, as
> long as we don't hit any serious production delays.

The point is, report language need not be stilted and formal.
There's a definite benefit to brightening it up a little. The purpose of
reports is to communicate facts clearly, preferably in an interesting
way. If your material is interesting to the audience he will retain
more, and have a more favorable impression of your work.

*(Continued on page 125.)*

The casual style is one way to add interest. Another way is what we call "readability,"—is the report easy to read, or hard to read? Factors in readability include everything from the subject matter (simple or complex), through organization and arrangement on the typed page, to length of paragraphs, sentences, and words. The most critical factor, though, is the last—the way you use words, sentences, and paragraphs.

There are a good many readability formulas, most of which involve considerable time spent in counting words, syllables, even suffixes. We're going to boil them down to three basic rules of thumb, which will show you when you are writing "hard-to-read" prose.

1. Not more than 25 percent of the words should have more than two syllables.

2. Sentences should have no more than 25 words.

3. Paragraphs should have no more than 150 words.

These rules define the outer limits of readability. If you exceed these limits, you can be sure your material is hard to read; the greater the excess, the greater the difficulty.

Memorize the three rules, then turn to page 127.

We've talked in general terms so far. Now let's deal specifically
with the kinds of words to use in reports, and the kind of words to
avoid. Good report style, whether formal or casual, uses short, simple words wherever possible. A report is not a showcase for the fruits
of your vocabulary-building efforts. It's great to know a lot of words,
but greater to know when not to use them. If the precise meaning
you want to convey can be expressed by only one six-syllable word,
go ahead and use it. Usually, though, you'll have a choice between
a longer, more impressive word and a shorter, more familiar one.
It's a sad truth that many report writers, especially members of the
ornate school, love to use the long word.

Look at these words:

> administrate
> cultivatable
> experimentalize
> filtrate (verb)
> preventative

What's wrong with them?

**1.** You're playing games—there's nothing wrong with those words.
**Page 119**
**2.** They are basically good words, but extra syllables or letters
have been thrown in.    **Page 129**
**3.** They're misspelled forms of good words.    **Page 130**

You won't have to check every paragraph you write against the three rules of thumb. It's a good idea, though, to check every so often, especially when the subject matter is difficult, to be sure you're staying in bounds.

Now write the three rules of thumb, and check your answer on page 136.

**128**   FROM PAGE 138

1. The bad word here is "percentage." "Number" says the same thing, in one less syllable. And, for that matter, why not "few" instead of "very small number"? We wind up with,

> *Only a few of the men were casualties.*

2. The weak spot is "meticulously." Why not say,

> *The good journalist is completely accurate.*

3. The word to get rid of is "pronunciamentos." It's better to say,

> *The congressman's career in the legislature was notable because of his flowery language* (or, *speech*).

Once again, let's repeat our principle: Say what you have to say briefly, using the simplest, most specific words that will get your meaning across.

Rewrite the following paragraph, in the clearest way you can, using the most accurate words you can think of.

The committee's extensive perusal of factors involved in the precipitous increase of terminations, both company- and employee-instigated, reveals that the preponderance of terminations can be attributed to employee dissatisfaction with the company's wage scale, which is 13 percent below the average for the industry, as well as being 19 percent below that of our principal local competitor in the field. It is our recommendation that the pay scales be realigned upward, to a level at least 13 percent in advance of the existing one, preferably 19 percent or more.

When you have rewritten the paragraph, compare it with ours on page 140.

*They are basically good words, but unnecessary syllables or letters have been added.*

Right. These forms demonstrate what happens when the writer isn't sure of the correct form—he pads the word, to make it sound more authoritative. The real words are:

| | |
|---|---|
| administrate | *administer* |
| cultivatable | *cultivable* |
| experimentalize | *experiment* |
| filtrate | *filter* |
| preventative | *preventive* |

A more common form of the long-word fever involves the use of a long word purely for effect when a good short word is available. In which of the following sentences, do you think you can make this criticism?

1. His chances for success in the election are improved by his knowledge of the mentality of the average native.

2. If we utilize all available resources, success is assured.

3. Only a small proportion of the population can read and write.

**1.** All of them.    **Page 138**
**2.** Sentences 1 and 3.    **Page 135**
**3.** Sentences 2 and 3.    **Page 132**

*They're misspelled forms of good words.*

No, we've spelled them correctly, and these spellings have wide usage. It's the forms themselves that are questionable.

Go back to page 126 and make another selection.

*Both sentences express opinions, but Sentence 2 contains loaded words.*

Right. The second sentence contains the term "creeping socialism," which definitely falls into the "loaded" category. "Creeping" has unpleasant associations for most people, and "socialism" is in very bad repute in America in the 1960's. And how would you define "creeping socialism"? Some might say it's "what the Democrats are doing to us"—but is that a factual definition? By saying that medical care for the aged is creeping socialism, we discredit it in purely emotional terms. If, on the other hand, we could name four characteristics of socialism, and then show that all four were present in the medical care for the aged program, we'd have a better case. (But we'd still have to throw out that "creeping.")

To sum up, be sure to use terms that you can define *factually*.

Go to page 134.

*Sentences 2 and 3.*

So you think Sentence 1 is OK. No, it can be improved. Couldn't we just as easily say, "His chances for success in the election are improved by his knowledge of the native mind"?

Go back to page 129 and try again.

*Both sentences express opinions in factual terms.*

No, we don't think so. The second sentence contains the term "creeping socialism." Could you give a good, 10-word definition of just what that is? Remember, when the reader is asked to react to the symbol, rather than to a factual definition, the presentation is slanted.

Go back to page 146 and make the other selection.

Slanting can also be accomplished by using nonloaded words, but selecting the facts in such a way that only one side of a story is presented and a specific impression is created. This is not a matter of writing style, however, so we won't go into it here. Really slanted writing combines both techniques, sometimes with devastating effect. For example:

His face was unshaven, his coat worn and tattered.
He wore a short beard; his coat was worn, but spotless.

Both these sentences tell us basically the same facts: the fellow in question has facial hair, and a very old coat. But what a contrast there is between the impressions these two statements convey! The way in which the facts are presented makes all the difference. As a report writer, you must present facts in a way that lets the reader make up his own mind about them.

Rewrite the following sentences in "uncolored" prose.

1. The juggernaut from State College once again victimized the undermanned Tech squad, this time by the score of 47–6.
2. A thoroughgoing reappraisal of the facts of the case has caused us to make a fresh judgment on the matter.
3. Fourscore and seven years ago, our fathers brought forth upon this continent a new nation, . . .

After you have rewritten them in straightforward terms, turn to page 137.

*Sentences 1 and 3.*

No, I'm afraid you're wrong. You say that Sentence 2 contains no over-long words—but what about "utilize"? Wouldn't that sentence be improved if we said "If we use all available resources . . ."?

Go back to page 129 and make another selection.

1. *Not more than 25 percent of the words should have more than two syllables.*
2. *Sentences should not have more than 25 words.*
3. *Paragraphs should not have more than 150 words.*

If you wrote the three rules correctly, go to page 126; if not, start again on page 125.

1. *The score was State 47, Tech 6.*
2. *We've changed our minds.*
3. *The nation is 87 years old,* or, *The nation was founded 87 years ago.*

Those long sentences look pretty short when we restrict ourselves to the facts. You may have noticed that all three of them were written in ornate style, with loaded words added: "juggernaut, victimized, undermanned" in the first; "thoroughgoing reappraisal" and "fresh judgment" in the second. The third is just pure ornate style, with an attempt to stimulate a favorable reaction in "our fathers." You may comment that the last of these three examples has a pretty good reputation. Quite so, but *it's not a report.* What more affecting bit of oratory is there than, "Never in the course of human events have so many owed so much to so few." It's a magnificent summary of a pivotal period in history—but it isn't report language. As report writers, we have to forego grandeur of language, and be unemotional.

Can you rewrite the following sentence in good report style, removing the slanting and the emotionally loaded words and phrases?

My opponent in this campaign has persisted in allying himself with questionable elements, including, most importantly, those who are soft in their policies toward our greatest enemy in the world today; to put it bluntly, he has continually consorted with the sort of liberals and parlor pinks who would happily sell us down the river.

Try it, then turn to page 139.

*All of them.*

You're right. They all contain unnecessary long words. We can make these improvements:

1. His chances for success in the election are improved by his knowledge of the native *mind*.
2. If we *use* all available resources, success is assured.
3. Only a small *part* of the population can read and write.

The thing to remember is not to use a long word where a short one will do. Now rewrite the following sentences, substituting simple words for long ones where necessary.

1. Only a very small percentage of the men were casualties.
2. The good journalist is meticulously accurate.
3. The congressman's career in the legislature was notable because of the flowery language of his pronunciamentos on various subjects.

Write your improved versions of these sentences, then turn to page 128 and compare them with ours.

**139**

We hope that you gave up trying to make a factual statement out of that mass of words, and didn't put a single word on paper. If this was the case, very good. If you did rewrite the sentence, analyze your work and see how factual it really is.

This is as far as we will go with semantics. As we said, you can get a full course from Dr. Hayakawa's book *Language in Thought and Action*. But for the report writer, it's enough to be aware of the thing that can happen. Then, by concentrating on specific words, you can sidestep the problems.

Go to page 149.

*Here's our version of the paragraph:*

> The committee investigated the recent sharp rise in the number of employees leaving the company. Two types were studied: Employees who left of their own accord, and those who were laid off. The most important cause is low wages. Our firm pays, on the average, 13 percent less than the industry-wide average, and 19 percent less than our local competitor. To ease the situation, we recommend a pay increase of at least 13 percent, and preferably 19 percent or more.

Your paragraph doesn't have to match ours word for word. Just so you substituted simple words for long ones, we'll give you full credit.

The words you use have not only to be short and clear, but they must express accurately what you want to say. Unless you're hiding something, there's no good reason for using a general word (for instance, "hot") for a specific one (for instance, "368°F"). When accurate words are used in a good casual style, we really start to communicate. Compare these two paragraphs:

1. The next topic we will cover will be the modification in fire protection/prevention capability. About three months ago we conducted a survey (with the valuable assistance of the local firefighting company) and the results indicated that for our company it would be better if we used a different type of extinguisher. We began work on the changeover within a very short time thereafter, and within a month and a half nearly two-thirds of the conversions had been made to the new dry-chemical type. As of the first of next month, if work proceeds on schedule, the conversion job will have been completed.

2. In April, Art Wilder in the Plant Safety Dept. surveyed our fire protection equipment, with the aid of the Fort Penn Fire Department. On May 15 the Executive Committee approved their recommendation that we switch from soda-acid extinguishers to the dry-chemical type. The changeover began on June 1, and by July 15 was two-thirds complete; the scheduled finishing date is September 1.

*(Continued on page 141.)*

We won't bother asking you which makes better reading. That's obvious. We'll just pound home the point once more: Good writing of any type depends on specific detail. Generalizations are just so much fog. Make a real effort to burn off that fog by using specific words that express precisely the facts you want to convey.

Rewrite the following sentences; make up enough specific data to convert them into really meaningful statements.

1. The evaluation committee recommends that we purchase the new model stapler, because it handles several different sizes, it works faster, and it misses less frequently.
2. The accident occurred because the forklift truck didn't have enough space to turn around in. We should widen the passageway at that point so that it won't happen again.

Go to page 143 and compare your sentences with ours.

There is another way in which words can give us trouble. This is the case in which words look as though they have specific meanings, when actually they don't. The branch of science that deals with words and their meanings is called "semantics." For a thorough introduction to it, we recommend that you read *Language in Thought and Action,* by Dr. S. I. Hayakawa (New York: Harcourt, Brace and World, Inc., 1949). For our purposes, it will be enough to expose you to a few principles.

The most important single fact in the study of words is this: words are merely symbols. They represent things, but they are not the things they represent. When we use one of these symbols called words, we must be sure that our listener gives that symbol the same meaning we do. Suppose we say "dog" and we think "German shepherd," but he thinks "collie." No communication. This gets us back to the importance of accurate, specific words.

Which of the following words are accurate in this sense?

(1) Communist          (4) Republican
(2) Mt. Everest        (5) Mickey Mantle
(3) Free Enterprise System

**1.** The second and fifth.    **Page 146**
**2.** The third and fifth.     **Page 145**
**3.** None of them.    **Page 148**

*Here are our versions:*

1. The evaluation committee tested several models of staplers, and recommended purchase of the Apex Stapl-rite because it performed best in both areas tested:
   (a) It is the only model to handle ¼-in., ⅜-in. and ½-in. staples.
   (b) When set for automatic operation, it will operate 180 times a minute, 35 per minute more than any other of the four models tested.

2. The accident occurred because a 16-foot forklift truck was executing a 180° turn in an 18-foot passageway. The passageway should be widened at this point to at least 22 feet.

If your sentences agreed with ours in principle—that is, if you put specific measurements in place of estimates—go to page 142. If not, go to page 144.

Apparently you need a little more work on specific words. Try to improve on these sentences, again making up any data you want to add.

1. Because of the results of two surveys, one of night shift personnel and one of day shift personnel, the union representative has recommended that we increase the meal break and decrease the coffee break.
2. In regard to that short delivery we were supposed to have made last week, all I can tell you is that our records show that it was complete when it left our dock, so either the customer didn't check it in right, or something happened on the way.

Write your corrected sentences, then compare them with the ones on page 147.

*The third and fifth.*

Well, we agree about Number 5, but you're wrong on Number 3. "Mickey Mantle" is about as specific as you can get. When we say "Mickey Mantle" we can be fairly sure that most people (in the U.S. in the 1960's) will know what we're talking about. But how about Number 3? What can you really tell about the free enterprise system, except the fact that the U.S. is called one? We would have to define a few more terms (for instance, "monopoly," "closed shop") before we could agree on just what we meant by "free enterprise." To be accurate, a word should symbolize just one thing. We mentioned "collie." That's a good, accurate word if we're talking about breeds of dogs. If we're talking specifically about the collie next door, we'd have to say "Rover" to be sure we were accurate.

Go back to page 142 and make another selection.

*The second and fifth.*

Exactly. We can discuss these words with most people without more detailed definition. But we couldn't discuss the other three with *anybody* without defining more precisely just what each of these symbols meant to each party. You ask, how does this apply to report writing? In this way: If the words we use are not accurate in the semantic sense, our communication is not only faulty, it may be completely incorrect.

The intentional use of semantic confusion to create false impressions, is called "slanting." And words that are semantically inaccurate, like "Communist," "Republican," and "free enterprise," are called "loaded" words. They are "loaded" because the weight they carry is more emotional than factual. Look at those three. The word "Communist" creates a hostile reaction in the minds of most Americans; "free enterprise" elicits a favorable response; and, of course, "Republican" can go either way. But the reactions are almost entirely emotional—reactions to the symbol, rather than to any factual definition.

A report should not contain slanting or loaded words. If you are forced to use them, at least use them in the knowledge that you're not being entirely honest. Look at these sentences:

1. I am opposed to the administration program of medical care for the aged.
2. I am opposed to the kind of creeping socialism represented by the administration program for medical care for the aged.

What do you think?

1. Both sentences express opinions in factual terms.   **Page 133**
2. Both sentences express opinions, but Sentence 2 contains loaded words.   **Page 131**

*Here are our versions:*

1. Sam Horner, the Union Representative, says that his men want to decrease the coffee break from 15 to 10 minutes, and increase the meal break from 20 to 25 minutes, on both shifts. He made a survey which showed that 160 of 217 men on days, and 114 of 143 men on nights are in favor of the idea.

2. Ford Dogfood Company has made a claim that our delivery to them on October 17 was short two barrels of horse fetlocks. Our bill of lading number 115349, signed M. Lasky, shows that the shipment was complete when it left here.

Once again, you should have replaced the generalizations with facts.

Go to page 142.

*None of them.*

You're pretty hard to convince, accuracy-wise. We agree with you on "Communist," "Republican," and "free enterprise." All three of these would take some further definition before you could use them in a discussion. (For instance, do you mean a Chinese Communist, or a Russian Communist; a Goldwater Republican, or a Rockefeller Republican? And how "free" is our free enterprise system?) However, "Mt. Everest" is an accurate term—how many Mt. Everests are there? The same goes for "Mickey Mantle." Very few people who live in the U.S. in the 1960's would not recognize that term. You might insist that we say "the Mickey Mantle who plays for the New York Yankees"—but unless we were talking about some other Mickey Mantle, it's not really necessary to name which one.

Go back to page 142 and make another selection.

Now that you've learned something about words and what they can do, it's time to look at sentences.

In case you're wondering, we're not going into a full-fledged grammar session; there are plenty of good books around for that. Any time you feel you need a review, stop the program; read a text on English grammar, and then come back to the point where you left off.

The first thing for you to remember is *keep it simple.* You might impress someone with long, complicated sentences if he's the type to be swayed by gobbledygook, but most people will be grateful for the consideration you show them if you express yourself clearly and briefly. As we told you in the section on words, beginning report writers think they have to get overly formal in their language when they write reports.

You can avoid complicated sentences by splitting them up into shorter ones. Here's a very poor sentence:

The rate of production for the latest fiscal year is higher than that of the previous year because this was the year that the new, automatic, high-speed, hydraulic stamping machines were installed, thus increasing the number of forms stamped over the period, as well as being the year that new time-saving and work-saving methods were introduced, also contributing to the higher production rate.

Let's rewrite it.

The production rate for the latest fiscal year is higher than the previous year. New automatic, high-speed, hydraulic stamping machines were installed, and new time- and work-saving methods were introduced. Both improvements increased the number of forms stamped during the period.

Note that we've split it into three short sentences. However, you don't want to overdo a good thing. The paragraph at the top of the next page does just that.

*(Continued on page 150.)*

In August the Ajax Toy Co. sold 50,000 yo-yos. By Christmas, sales reached three times that. During January sales dropped to 1000 yo-yos. In February and March sales increased to 5000. April sales reached 10,000. May and June showed a rise to 20,000.

Notice that it is boring, repetitious, and reads in a choppy manner because you have a whole string of short sentences. We don't want you to end up with a short, staccato style; therefore, you should vary the length of your sentences. Do keep them short and simple, as we've already told you, but vary the length. Let's rewrite the paragraph shown above.

In August the Ajax Toy Co. sold 50,000 yo-yos. By Christmas, sales reached three times that. During January sales dropped to 1000, but increased to 5000 during February and March. April sales reached 10,000, and May and June showed a rise to 20,000.

As you can see, the sentences are still short, but they are varied in length. Some are very short; some a little longer. The original paragraph also illustrates another fault in style: notice that we plodded along subject-verb, subject-verb. That is as deadly as a series of short sentences. Don't be guilty of this fault either—vary the style of your sentences.

*Rule 1:* Keep it short and simple.
*Rule 2:* Vary the length of your sentences.
*Rule 3:* Don't use a whole string of short sentences together.
*Rule 4:* Vary the style of your sentences.

Which of these rules does the following group of sentences violate?

The experiment was started in January. The apparatus was put together in six weeks. At that time the synthesizing process began. The synthetic chemicals were separated. Then they were used in tests on white mice.

1. Rule 2.        **Page 158**
2. Rule 3.        **Page 152**
3. Rules 2, 3, and 4.        **Page 160**
4. Rules 2 and 3.        **Page 154**
5. Rule 4.        **Page 156**

*Short sentences are better than long ones.*

Oh no. Where were you when we told you to keep it simple?

Go back to page 150 for a review, then return to page 157 and select the right answer.

*Rule 3.*

This is partially correct, but did you forget the other rules we showed you?

Reread pages 149–150 and choose the right answer from page 150.

*Vary the length of your sentences.*

No, you are wrong. Go back to page 150 for a review, then return to page 157 and choose the right answer.

*Rules 2 and 3.*

You've almost got it right, but you forgot some of what we told you.

Review pages 149–150, then choose the right answer on page 150.

"Keep it short and simple" is the one rule not violated on page 150. If you didn't know this, better review pages 149–150. If you did know it, continue reading.

Let's talk more about varying the form of your sentences. Try an inverted order occasionally, such as, "Before the flood, Noah built the Ark." Or this one: "During the audit, the accountants found discrepancies in the books." See what we mean?

Try rewriting this series of sentences. Remember to apply all the rules you've learned so far.

Copper is well known as an excellent conductor. It oxidizes at slightly elevated temperatures. Copper wire, therefore, is constantly reduced in size because of the oxidizing action. Enamel coating on the wire is damaged by this reducing action.

Turn to page 157 and compare your sentences with ours.

*Rule 4.*

No, you are only partly correct. True, this rule is violated, but it is not the only one.

Return to pages 149–150, reread them, and select the correct answer on page 150.

*Your sentences should resemble these:*

Copper, well known as an excellent conductor, oxidizes at slightly elevated temperatures. Because of the oxidizing action, therefore, copper wire is constantly reduced in size, damaging the enamel coating on the wire.

Which one of the following rules of sentence structure *haven't* we discussed?

1. Short sentences are better than long ones.   **Page 151**
2. Vary the length of your sentences.   **Page 153**
3. Don't use run-on sentences.   **Page 159**
4. Don't use a whole string of short sentences together.
   **Page 164**
5. Vary the style of your sentences.   **Page 162**

*Rule 2.*

This answer is partly right, but what about the other rules we've taught you?

Reread pages 149–150, and then pick the correct answer on page 150.

*Don't use run-on sentences.*

That answer is correct. You probably remember this rule from your high-school grammar. That's why we didn't teach it.

We've told you to keep your sentences short, but exactly how *do* you make them short? One way is to cut out unnecessary words. For example, instead of saying "The accountants were allowed a period of three months to complete the audit of the books," say "The accountants were allowed three months to complete the audit."

Which of the following sentences is written as compactly as possible?

1. The supervisor was waiting for the report in a state of impatience.   **Page 163**
2. The process of manufacturing television sets is complicated. **Page 161**
3. After being polished, the steel ball bearings ran at maximum speed.   **Page 165**

*Rules 2, 3, and 4.*

Absolutely right! That paragraph violates every rule we've taught you about sentences except one, and you should know what that is by process of elimination. State it here, then go to.page 155.

*The process of manufacturing television sets is complicated.*

No. This sentence can be shortened to: "The manufacture of television sets is complicated."

Return to page 159 and pick another answer.

*Vary the style of your sentences.*

No, that is not right. We told you to vary the style of your sentences back on page 150.

Return to page 150 for a review, then go back to page 157 and pick the right answer.

*The supervisor was waiting for the report in a state of impatience.*

That is wrong. It can be shortened to this: "The supervisor waited impatiently for the report."

Now go back to page 159 and select another answer.

*Don't use a whole string of short sentences together.*

Oh no. We *did* tell you that on page 150.

Go back to page 150 for a review, then return to page 157 and choose the right answer.

*After being polished, the steel ball bearings ran at maximum speed.*

Right you are! You didn't let the inverted order fool you. This sentence is as short as possible.

Here are examples of ways to cut sentences.

| *Don't say:* | *When you can say:* |
|---|---|
| along the lines of | like |
| due to the fact that | because |
| with reference to | about |
| prior to | before |
| in the future | (leave out when verb is in future tense) |
| | |
| be in a position to | can |
| during the course of | during |
| in the state of Maine | in Maine |
| in the city of Los Angeles | in Los Angeles |
| during the year 1964 | during 1964 |

Look through your own writing and you can find similar examples.

Applying these rules, rewrite this sentence:

In the years 1950 to 1960, the City of Los Angeles in the State of California began to undergo a large phase of expansion because of the influx of many people arriving from the east to make a home and live there.

Go to page 166.

*Your sentence should look something like this:*

During 1950–1960, the population of Los Angeles, California began to increase rapidly because of the influx of people who moved there from the east.

If it doesn't, check your sentence to see where you used more words than necessary. Refer back to the list on page 165 if need be.

Different parts of a sentence that are related to each other must be stated in the same way. If you use a word like "describ*ing*," you must use a word like "explain*ing*." An example of this is:

The school board sent out pamphlets *which explained* the new school building program and *which showed* how taxpayers' dollars were to be spent.

A wrong way of writing this sentence would be:

The school board sent out pamphlets *which explained* the new school building program and *showing* how the taxpayers' dollars were to be spent.

Now you try rewriting this sentence (disregard length for the moment):

Factory operations have proved that sodium chloride is a useful compound and its economy.

Which of these rewritten versions is correct?

**1.** Factory operations have proved that sodium chloride is a useful compound and that it is economical.     **Page 168**
**2.** Factory operations have proved that sodium chloride is both useful and economical.     **Page 172**
**3.** Both sentences are correct.     **Page 171**

*Sentence 1.*

Good, you've picked it up well. Go to page 176.

*Sentence 1.*

That's partly right, but remember that the English language offers wide latitude of expression and there's more than one way to be correct.

Return to page 166 and check another answer.

*Sentence 1.*

That's right. Evidently you remember the difference between the active and passive voice.

Go on to new material on page 176.

*Sentence 2.*

This is incorrect. Sentence 2 is already written in the active voice; that is, the subject of the sentence is doing the action or activity. Decide what the subject of your sentence is and determine whether it is performing the activity or if the activity is being performed on it.

Try again. Which sentence is in the active voice?

1. The factory installed a new production line last week. **Page 167**
2. During installation of the production line, ten new machines were added.     **Page 173**

*Both sentences are correct.*

That's right. Remember we told you there's more than one way to be correct when you're dealing with sentence structure.

Sentences can be lively or dull. One way to ensure lively sentences is by making sure that verbs are active, not passive. Some people have the mistaken impression that putting a sentence in the passive voice lends dignity to a report. Remember that the simplest sentences consistent with the material you are presenting are best.

Which sentence would you change to the active voice?

1. The books were examined by the government auditor and were given formal approval with a few changes. **Page 169**
2. The test engineer examined the blueprints and returned them to the draftsman for corrections. **Page 170**

*Sentence 2.*

You are partly right, but don't forget what we've told you about great variety of expression in English.

Return to page 166 and check another answer.

*Sentence 2.*

We're sorry, but you probably let the clause at the beginning fool you. The machines were added. That is, some one or something *added* the machines to the assembly line.

Here's one more example: "The hen laid an egg." That's active. "The egg was laid by the hen." That's passive.

Now try again, and get it right this time. Pick the active sentence:

**1.** The project was started by the manager in January.
**Page 174**

**2.** The manager started the project in January.      **Page 177**

*The project was started by the manager in January.*

Sorry, you're wrong. We think you need the grammar review we mentioned earlier. Get a textbook on English, study it, then return to page 176 in the program.

*Sentence 1.*

No, you are wrong. We said that the different parts of a sentence should agree in time. Sentence 1 said "are available" in the first part and "they hadn't" in the second part. Those two don't agree; one is in the present tense and the other is in the past tense.

Now go back to page 182 and choose the correct answer.

When you are constructing sentences, beware of misplacing words. Sometimes very amusing things happen when you put them in the wrong place. For example:

Walking down the street, the building was clearly visible.

How many times have *you* seen a building walking down the street?

Now, what do you think of the following sentence?

Sparkling in the sunlight, we saw the lake as we climbed the hill.

**1.** It should be rewritten.     **Page 181**
**2.** There's nothing wrong with it.     **Page 178**

*The manager started the project in January.*

Very good. Now you've learned it. Go to page 176.

*There's nothing wrong with it.*

No, you are wrong. As the sentence is written, you can't tell which is sparkling in the sunlight, "we" or "the lake." Now how about rewriting the following sentence:

When ill on the job, the company medical facility will take care of you.

When _____ _____ ill on the job, the company medical facility will take care of you.

Go to page 180.

*The men stopped the machines while they were stamping the dies,* or
*The men stopped the machines which were stamping the dies.*

Now how about this sentence?

Although recently overhauled, the metal resisted cutting by the machine.

**1.** It should be rewritten.
**2.** It is OK.

Take your pick and go on to page 181.

*When you are ill on the job, the company medical facility will take care of you.*

Rewrite this sentence:

While stamping the dies, the men stopped the machines.

Go to page 179.

*It should be rewritten.*

That's right.

So that you really appreciate how important it is to place a word as close as possible to the word it modifies, look at this sentence just for fun.

He told her that he loved her.

We'll place the word "only" in every possible position in this sentence. See what it does to the meaning every time.

*Only* he told her that he loved her.
He *only* told her that he loved her.
He told *only* her that he loved her.
He told her *only* that he loved her.
He hold her that *only* he loved her.
He told her that he *only* loved her.
He told her that he loved *only* her.
He told her that he loved her *only*.

Go on to page 182.

The time sense of a sentence is important to its impact on the reader. Even though the report you are writing covers a period of time, you can often put your sentences in the present tense. For example:

Production figures *show* that production *is* higher this year than last.

Don't say,

Production figures *showed* that production *was* higher this year than last.

The different parts of a sentence should also agree in their use of time. Take your choice between these two sentences.

1. Although cost control figures are available for fiscal 1964, they were not compiled.     **Page 175**
2. Although cost control figures are available for fiscal 1964, they haven't yet been compiled.     **Page 185**

FROM PAGES 185, 186

**183**

*Sentence 1.*

You are absolutely correct. Not only does the pronoun follow closely after the words it stands for, but, because it is a plural pronoun, there is no doubt what those words are. If you don't feel secure in your handling of pronouns go to page 186; otherwise, continue reading.

Now, we're going to tackle a point that has probably caused more grief than any other, and needlessly. Making the verb and the subject agree is really not the bugaboo most people think it is. The trick is not to let the words between the subject and the verb fool you into changing the verb. Let's look at a sample of what we mean.

A package containing several books *was* handed to him.

Note that it is *was,* not *were.* Just forget the words "containing several books" and pretend the sentence reads "A package was handed to him." You wouldn't have any trouble at all with that sentence, now would you? Look at another example:

Parts for the new motor were shipped from the warehouse.

See? Here the verb is plural because the subject is plural. Forget the words "for the new motor."

Now you try a couple. Tell which sentences are correct.

1. The hoist crane carrying several tons was put into standby operation.
2. The project director, along with his subordinates, was going to Washington for a meeting with the U.S. Air Force.
3. The manager and his assistant were planning the budget allotment for the production department.

**1.** All three are correct.　　**Page 190**
**2.** Sentence 3 is wrong, the others correct.　　**Page 195**
**3.** Sentence 2 is wrong, the others correct.　　**Page 189**
**4.** Sentence 1 is wrong, the others correct.　　**Page 193**

*Sentence 2.*

No, we're sorry, but you aren't right. This sentence is ambiguous, because you don't know which are at peak production.

Return to page 185 and select another answer.

*Sentence 2.*

Of course. The two parts of the sentence must agree. If you are talking about present events, stay in the present; if you must use the past, stay in the past.

Another useful rule for good sentences is avoid pronouns when you can. (Pronouns: *I, we, he, she, it, they, me, us, him, her, them,* etc.) Confusion can develop if you use pronouns. For example:

When the engineer tried to seat the tube into its socket, he found it was too large.

Which was too large, the tube or the socket? Probably the socket, because the pronoun follows immediately afterwards; but you can't be sure. Instead, restate it in this form or some similar one:

When the engineer tried to insert the tube, he found the socket was too large.

No confusion now.

If you must use pronouns, use them carefully, especially *it, they,* and *them,* and be sure the words referred to are immediately before the pronouns.

Choose the best among these sentences:

1. The president of the company received the estimate and the budget in time for the board meeting, and they were well received.   **Page 183**
2. New factories were constructed to build aircraft precision parts, and now they are at peak production.   **Page 184**
3. The machines produced 200 sprockets an hour; they were highly polished.   **Page 187**

So you want more review? Fine. The key to this whole thing is making sure your audience knows what you're referring to. If you're not sure they will, use the technique you learned back in Chapter 3: have someone else read your sentence to see if he understands it.

Pronouns stand for something else; there must be no doubt in anyone's mind what that something else is. Remember not to use pronouns unless you must to keep the sentences smooth-running, and remember, if you do use pronouns, to keep the words they refer to as close to the pronouns as possible. For example:

The accountant checked the budget figures and found they were correct.

Which one of these sentences is best?

1. The foreman inspected the finished assemblies and approved them for shipment.     **Page 183**
2. When the packages containing nuts and bolts were received, they were found to be defective.     **Page 191**
3. Finished assemblies and their housings are placed in crates, and then they are shipped to the customers.     **Page 188**

*Sentence 3.*

Oh come now, which were highly polished, the machines or the sprockets?

Go back to page 185 and try another answer.

*Sentence 3.*

That is incorrect. You should go to page 185 for a complete review.

*Sentence 2 is wrong, the others correct.*

No, you forgot what we said about dropping out the words between the subject and the verb. Look at the sentence this way:

The project director (along with his subordinates) was going to Washington for a meeting with the Air Force.

Go back, reread page 183, and then select another answer.

*All three are correct.*

That's right. Just keep one fact in mind: Select the subject of your sentence, drop out all words between the subject and the verb, and you'll automatically pick the correct form of the verb.

Let's talk briefly about sentence fragments. (Remember, this is not a grammar program. If you are on shaky ground, refer to a grammar textbook; then come back to the program.) Avoid sentence fragments at all times. You can recognize one in this way: If it stands by itself, it's a sentence. If it must lean upon the preceding or following sentence, it's a fragment. Fragments also betray themselves by words such as: *since, although, because, being, in, by,* and *through.*

Which of the following is *not* a fragment?

1. Inasmuch as the engineer planned his project.     **Page 194**
2. Because a contract was drawn, the project began.     **Page 192**
3. While the surveyors mapped the land and recorded their findings.     **Page 196**

*Sentence 2.*

No, you are wrong. Go to page 185 for a complete review.

*Because a contract was drawn, the project began.*

You're right, you didn't let the "because" fool you. This is a complete sentence. Its subject is the word "project," not the word "contract."

You get rid of a fragment by attaching it to the sentence before or after it, or by making it a complete sentence. For example, a fragment like "since the pipeline is a complicated piece of equipment" can be converted to a sentence such as:

However, the pipeline is a complicated piece of equipment.

Or, you can drop the "however" completely. Combining a fragment with another sentence is self-explanatory. The main thing is for you to be on the alert for fragments in your writing. Once you spot them, you'll easily find ways to get rid of them.

Go to page 197.

*Sentence 1 is wrong, the others correct.*

Wrong. Remember what we said about forgetting the words between the subject and the verb. Pretend the sentence reads like this: "The hoist crane (carrying several tons) was put into standby operation."

Reread page 183 and then select another answer.

*Inasmuch as the engineer planned his project.*

No. This *is* a fragment. You have to read the preceding or following sentence to find out what happened before or after the engineer planned the project.

Return to page 190 and pick the correct answer.

*Sentence 3 is wrong, the others correct.*

No. You probably didn't notice that the subject of the sentence is "The manager and his assistant." Therefore, the plural verb "were" is correct.

Return to page 183 and select another answer.

*While the surveyers mapped the land and recorded their findings.*

That's not correct. It *is* a fragment because it cannot stand alone—you have to find out what is happening "while the surveyors mapped . . ."

Go back to page 190 and select another answer.

Answer the following questions.

**1.** The first rule for the construction of good sentences is . . .

**2.** To avoid monotony, it is a good idea to vary sentence
(a) Style    (b) Length    (c) Style *and* length

**3.** Rewrite this sentence if necessary:
The rate of production of the Model A3 version of the new food mixer was higher after the factory employees were given hourly increases of $.15 per hour each.

**4.** Which of the following sentences is (are) in the passive voice?
(a) Laboratory experiments on new crystal diodes were terminated during the first week in May.
(b) The machines did not operate smoothly after they were started.
(c) No one noticed that they were late for the meeting.

**5.** True or false—This sentence is correct:
Each of the 500 employees in the building are eligible to use the new recreational facilities.

**6.** Related parts of a sentence must agree with each other in two ways. What are they?

**7.** Fix this sentence to read correctly:
Painting the house red we saw the man.

**8.** State whether or not these sentences are right and what to do about them if they are wrong.
The men carried briefcases filled with papers. They were important and were needed in Washington immediately.

**9.** True or false—This is a sentence fragment:
Even though he began the experiment soon enough to finish it on time.

**10.** True or false—Sentences should be short, simple, and similar to each other.

Turn to page 198 for the answers.

The answers to the questions are listed below. Next to each answer
is a page number. If you miss a question, go back to the page number shown for a review. If you score 100 percent, go on to page 201.

1. Keep it simple (or short).     **Page 149**
2. (c) Style *and* length.     **Page 149.**
3. Your sentence should read something like this:
   The production rate of the new Model A3 food mixer increased after all employees received a $.15 per hour salary
   increase.     **Page 159**
4. (a) and (b)     **Pages 171** and **173**
5. False; the verb should be singular.     **Page 183**
6. Word form must be alike (parallelism).     **Page 166**
   Tense must be alike (time).     **Page 182**
7. Either of the following:
   While we were painting the house red, we saw the man, or
   We saw the man painting the house red.     **Page 176**
8. The sentences are wrong. "They" in the second sentence has
   an ambiguous reference. You must specify what it refers back to.
   **Page 185**
9. True.     **Page 190**
10. False; not all the time.     **Page 149**

**PANEL 4–1**

An analog computer manipulates physical quantities that represent the mathematical variables of the particular problem under study. In the mechanical type of analog computer, for example, the machine variables may be rotating shafts driven by gear trains. The angular displacement of the shafts is measured to produce the solution to the equation or mathematical operation. Computers for solving navigation and bombing problems have used these principles for years. Early radar gun directors also made use of this type of operation. Although it is often called an analog computer or simulator, the computing elements are not usually direct analogs of the physical quantities in the problem. Instead, they are analogs of the mathematical equations describing the problem.

*Paragraph 1*

A digital computer, on the other hand, performs the required mathematical operations with numbers expressed in the form of digits. The machine essentially is composed of a number of counters which register and add in discrete or separate steps. Desk calculating machines are familiar forms of the mechanical type of digital computer. The first automatic sequence-controlled calculator used mechanical counters that were controlled by magnetic clutches and relays. International Business Machines Corporation began construction of this machine in 1939.

*Paragraph 2*

Later, electronic digital computers were developed, starting with the Electrical Numerical Integrator and Calculator (ENIAC). This machine was the first to use electronic circuits as the actual computing elements. It was designed primarily for step-by-step numerical integration of the equations of external ballistics. Although this computer used a scale of ten, the airborne digital computers used in missiles today operate on the binary system of numbers. Refer to Appendix A for a discussion of binary numbers.

*Paragraph 3*

## PANEL 4–2

Computer units in guided missile systems are found in various forms. A computer unit may be simple, such as a mixing circuit in an airborne vehicle; or it may be complex, as in a large-scale ground installation where the complete flight of a missile is determined. Whether airborne or ground-based, the computer unit is related to other guidance units as shown in Figure 1.

*Paragraph 1*

Reliability of guided missile operation can be developed and maintained only by the process of exposing the missile's many components to an exhaustive testing program. Also, margins of safety between service and working conditions must be established. The extreme conditions which cause individual components to fail must similarly be determined.

*Paragraph 2*

In the body of this report, some systems are covered for background purposes only. As systems evolve, the old ones become obsolete. Even so, the present systems are worthy of consideration in the interests of understanding the reasons for trends in present-day circuits.

*Paragraph 3*

This does not mean, however, that equipment will become increasingly complicated. A combination of theoretical principles and manufacture of accurate components will eliminate certain refinements in present circuits. These refinements exist only to compensate for possible signal errors in the first place. An uncomplicated, accurate system is the anticipated research and development goal.

*Paragraph 4*

Panel 4–1 (page 199) shows three sample paragraphs from the body of a report. Notice that the paragraphs are approximately 100 words long (within 20 percent). This is a good rule of thumb to remember, along with the 150-word maximum we taught you before. If your paragraphs run above 150 words or are much below 100 words, examine them carefully. If they are too long, they may have more than one main thought. If they are too short, make sure that you didn't continue the main thought into the next paragraph. If you did, then combine the two paragraphs. Beware, however, of arbitrarily combining paragraphs just because they are short ones. Notice that paragraphs in Panel 4–2 (opposite page) are less than 100 words long, but they are long enough for the simple thoughts they convey. On the other hand, if you have a complicated thought to explore, a long paragraph is necessary. That's why the lengths stated above are only recommendations.

Your paragraph length will be determined by what?

1. The type of report you're writing.     **Page 206**
2. The difficulty or simplicity of your main thought.     **Page 204**
3. The type of audience you're writing for.     **Page 203**
4. How many words it takes to express your main thought adequately.     **Page 205**

Look at Paragraph 2 in Panel 4–2 (page 200). What is the basic thought in that paragraph?

When you have decided what it is, turn to page 208.

*The type of audience you're writing for.*

No, that is not completely right. Although we told you the audience shapes everything you write, there are other considerations. Even when writing for the largest possible audience you may need long paragraphs at times. On the other hand, complicated technical reports will require short paragraphs for simple thoughts.

Return to page 201 and choose the right answer.

*The difficulty or simplicity of your main thought.*

Right you are. Difficult thoughts take more words to express them properly, whereas simple thoughts require fewer words. That's why you would also have been right if you had chosen the answer "How many words it takes to express your main thought adequately."

Go to page 202.

*How many words it takes to express your main thought adequately.*

That's correct. If you have a complicated thought, you will have a longer paragraph; a simple thought will require a shorter paragraph. You would also have been correct if you had chosen the answer "The difficulty or simplicity of your main thought."

Go to page 202.

*The type of report you're writing.*

No, that is not correct. Even a highly technical report will have short paragraphs. Conversely, a report written for popular consumption can have long paragraphs.

Return to page 201 and select the correct answer.

*Fourth (or last).*

The rest of the sentences in the paragraph all lead up to the last sentence, which is the *main* sentence in this case.

Complete this statement:

The _____ sentence must express the subject of the paragraph and the attitude to be taken toward it if there is one.

Go to page 209.

*The need for testing program to determine reliability* (or some similar phrase).

The rest of the paragraph all enlarges on this main idea.

Now look at Paragraph 2 of Panel 4–2 again. What is the main sentence of the paragraph?

    **1.** First sentence.
    **2.** Second sentence.
    **3.** Third sentence.

Go to page 210.

*Main (or topic).*

Is the following a good main sentence?

This causes a regular variation in the flux density to be established, inducing an AC voltage in the coils.

Go to page 211.

*First sentence.*

This sentence is the bones of the paragraph. The rest are the flesh that fills out the bones.

The main thought in Paragraph 4 of Panel 4–2 is which sentence?

When you have decided what it is, turn to page 207.

*No.*

It refers *back* to the main sentence. The word "this" linked the sentence with the previous one, or as we say, provided a transition. Some transitional elements are: *however, besides, because, consequently, therefore, on the other hand, nevertheless.* You can probably think of others.

Look at Paragraph 1 of Panel 4–1. There are three transitional elements here: "for example," "although it," and "instead." How many are there in Paragraph 2 of Panel 4–1?

Go to page 213.

*4, 2, 3, 1.*

Write a paragraph using the following facts:

Engineering produced simplified designs for manufacturing.
A new manufacturing process was introduced.
Production was higher this year than it was last year.
The employees' morale increased; so did their production rate.

Go to page 214.

*One* ("on the other hand").

Now look at Paragraph 3 in Panel 4–1. It contains _____ (how many?) transitions.

Go to page 215.

*Here is our version:*

Production is higher this year than last year for three reasons: engineering produced simplified designs for a new manufacturing process; the new manufacturing process was introduced; and employee morale increased during the year, raising the production rate.

Your paragraph doesn't have to match exactly, but you should have the main thought first and you should have seen the logical progression of ideas. If you didn't, better review from page 114. Otherwise proceed to page 216.

*Three* ("later," "it," "although").

Arrange these sentences into a paragraph (list by number).

1. Someday, whole factories will be automated to the point where the machinery will even repair itself, eliminating humans from the manufacturing chain entirely.
2. Because of this, engineers are constantly seeking ways to automate portions of factories that were thought impossible only a few years ago.
3. Today, entire assembly lines can be made to function without human intervention at any stage in the assembly process.
4. Automatic manufacturing, or automation, is the trend in all types of industries.

Go to page 212.

**216**

When you make an important point, you want your audience to notice it. In reports it isn't good usage to use exclamation points, and you can't decorate your text with attention-getters like a different-colored ink. So, how <u>do</u> you emphasize important points? (*Hint:* we just showed you one way—look at the word "do" just preceding.) However, this method should be used sparingly and only for one or two words at a time. Your best bet is in the placement of the statements you wish to emphasize.

Where would you place a sentence you want to call attention to?

1. At the beginning of a paragraph.   **Page 218**
2. In the middle of a paragraph.   **Page 221**
3. At the end of a paragraph.   **Page 219**

*Placement of the main sentence first.*

Your answer is partly right. One method of emphasis here is the placement of the main sentence first. Now go back to page 220 and pick the right answer.

*At the beginning of a paragraph.*

You are right. The beginning of a paragraph is one place you would put a sentence you wish to emphasize. However, you would also have been right if you had chosen the answer "At the end of a paragraph," because either answer is correct.

Go on to page 220.

*At the end of a paragraph.*

Yes. This device is often used for emphasis; however, you would also have been correct if you had selected the answer "At the beginning of a paragraph," because either answer is right.

Go on to page 220.

to what we said about paragraphing. Remember the
_e? That's generally the sentence you want to emphasize.
, it usually comes at the beginning of a paragraph. How-
is also effective to put it at the end of a paragraph and have
an _ sentences lead up to it. Look at Paragraph 3 in Panel 4–2
(page 200). The main sentence is the last one; it is placed there for
emphasis. By placing the main sentence at the end of a paragraph
occasionally, you avoid being in a rut.

Examine this paragraph:

In the automation field, engineers are concentrating on developing sophisticated control devices. Control devices start and stop
the automated factory upon command. Control devices are responsible for the action of computers, and someday, control devices will
perform many different tasks in the home.

What do you think is the attention-getter here?

1. Placement of the main sentence first.     **Page 217**
2. Repetition of the words "control devices."     **Page 222**
3. Both of the above.     **Page 229**

*In the middle of the paragraph.*

That is not correct. If you put the sentence in the middle of the paragraph, you will lose it there.

Go back to page 216 and choose the correct answer.

*Repetition of the words "control devices."*

You're almost right. Repetition of the words "control devices" is one of the methods of emphasis in this paragraph.

Go back to page 220 and choose the correct answer.

*8, 3, 1, 2, 4, 5, 6, 7.*

No, you have it backwards. The least important things about the V-1 are its weight and what the V-1 stands for.

Go back to page 216 and review from there.

*Example 1.*

You fell into our trap. This assignment is fine for the items under part I-A in Panel 4–3, but what about part I-B? What will you do with the fourth-level headings?

Go back to page 226 and pick the correct answer.

*7, 6, 4, 5, 8, 1, 2, 3.*

Absolutely right. The most important thing about the V-1 was that it caused great damage and lowered morale. The least important thing is that V-1 stands for Vengence Weapon No. 1. It's nice information to know, but it is not necessary for an understanding or history of the weapon.

When you are writing the body of a long report, it's generally a good idea to break up the text into sections. This makes for easier reading. You identify these sections by using headings, much as a newspaper story has a headline at the beginning of a story and smaller headlines in the body. Your company or school may have its own style for headings. If so, do as they do. Continue with this portion of the program, but find a sample report to compare what we say with that style. If you are not bound to a particular style, follow what we say here.

## THIS IS A SECTION HEADING

## THIS IS A MAJOR HEADING

### This is a Second-Level Heading

### This is a Third-Level Heading

You shouldn't need more than these four levels of headings. If you need only three, omit the section heading and start with the major heading.

You will find that your report breaks up naturally into subdivisions. It's at these subdivisions that you assign headings. To find them you need only look back at the outline you prepared for your report.

*(Continued on page 226.)*

Look at Panel 4–3 (opposite page) for a sample outline that will lend itself to assignment of headings. Figure out how many levels of headings you will need and assign them accordingly. Then choose the correct assignment of headings below.

**1.** HISTORY OF ROCKETS

<u>Birth of Guided Missiles</u>
World War I
Post-War
World War II                                                    **Page 224**

**2.**                     HISTORY  OF  ROCKETS

BIRTH  OF  GUIDED  MISSILES

<u>World War I</u>
<u>Post-War</u>
<u>World War II</u>                                              **Page 228**

**PANEL 4–3**

I. History of Rockets

  A. Birth of Guided Missiles
    1. World War I
    2. Post-War
    3. World War II
    4. Reaction-type Engines

  B. American Rocketry
    1. Dr. Goddard's Contribution
      a. Early Experiments
      b. Later Modifications
    2. American Rocket Society

  C. German Rocketry
    1. Peenemünde Project
    2. World War II Developments

II. Evolution of Jet Engines

  A. Early Experiments

  B. World War II
    1. American Development
    2. German Development

*Example 2.*

You're right. You need four levels of headings to be able to include everything under part I-B in Panel 4–3, even though you need only three levels for part I-A.

Keep them short! That's the cardinal rule in writing headings. As with many of the other things we have discussed, there is no one right way to write headings. Just remember to make them as short as possible.

Another rule to remember is: make headings on the same level alike. Look at the samples below and pick the one you think is correct.

**1.** Testing Chemicals
   Chemical Composition          **Page 236**

**2.** Testing of Chemicals
   Composition of Chemicals      **Page 232**

**3.** Chemical Tests
   Chemical Composition          **Page 234**

*Both of the above.*

That's correct. The repetition of the words "control devices" serves to emphasize the subject of the paragraph. The emphasis was first placed on control devices by using those words in the main sentence of the paragraph, the first sentence. Then the repetition served further to emphasize the subject of the paragraph.

How would you arrange the following facts, putting the proper emphasis on each so as to interest the widest possible audience?

1. The V-1 rocket was a pilotless monoplane.
2. The V-1 had a conventional airframe and tail construction.
3. V-1 stands for Vengence Weapon No. 1.
4. The V-1 was not accurate.
5. The V-1 could be shot down easily.
6. V-1 damage to London caused low morale.
7. The V-1 created great physical damage.
8. The V-1 warhead weighed 1988 pounds.

Arrange the numbers in order of emphasis, greatest first.

**1.** 8, 3, 1, 2, 4, 5, 6, 7.     **Page 223**
**2.** 7, 6, 4, 5, 8, 1, 2, 3.     **Page 225**
**3.** 4, 5, 1, 2, 8, 6, 7, 3.     **Page 230**

**230**

*4, 5, 1, 2, 8, 6, 7, 3.*

No, this is not correct. You emphasized design details that would be most important only to a specialized audience.

Go back to page 229 and choose the right answer.

Producing the Saline Solution
Defining of Electrolysis

No. You remembered the rule about making the headings alike. However, they must also be appropriate. "Defining of Electrolysis" is an awkward construction and poor form for a report.

Return to page 234 and choose another answer.

Testing of Chemicals
Composition of Chemicals

No. You remembered the rule about making headings alike, but you forgot that they should be as short as possible.

Go back to page 228 and select another answer.

Production of Saline Solution
Definition of Electrolysis

Absolutely right! These match each other and they are appropriate for a report.

Now choose the correct order of headings from the groupings shown below.

**1.**                     EMPLOYEE RETIREMENT PLAN

Basic Considerations
Dollar Expenditures
ELIGIBLE EMPLOYEES                                   **Page 235**

**2.**                     EMPLOYEE RETIREMENT PLAN

BASIC CONSIDERATIONS
Dollar Expenditures
Eligible Employees                                   **Page 238**

**3.**                     EMPLOYEE RETIREMENT PLAN

Basic Considerations
DOLLAR EXPENDITURES

ELIGIBLE EMPLOYEES

                                                     **Page 242**

**234**                                                    FROM PAGE 228

Chemical Tests
Chemical Composition

You are correct. The form of equal weight headings must be the
same, and they should be as short as possible.

Now try another one:

1. Producing the Saline Solution
   Defining of Electrolysis      **Page 231**

2. Production of Saline Solution
   Defining Electrolysis      **Page 237**

3. Production of Saline Solution
   Definition of Electrolysis      **Page 233**

*Example 1.*

No. The major, second-, and third-level headings are backwards.

Go back to page 225 for a review.

<u>Testing Chemicals</u>
<u>Chemical Composition</u>

That's not right. The headings should be alike.

Go back to page 228, review what we said, and select another answer.

Production of Saline Solution
Defining Electrolysis

No. You are wrong. When you use -*ing* for one heading, you 'must use -*ing* for the other headings of the same weight or level.

Go back to page 234 and pick another answer.

*Example 2.*

That's correct. You remembered what we told you back on page 225.

Now read pages 239–241. Write in headings where you think they should go, then turn to page 243.

Just as World War II was not fought along the same lines as World War I, victory in a future war will not be realized by World War II aircraft practices. However, the solution of guided missile problems of the future will stem from past experiences. If anyone is to profit from the lessons learned from the missiles of the past, these lessons must be analyzed and applied in the light of the current situation.

The idea of guided missiles was born during World War I. The use of the airplane as a military weapon brought about considerable thought concerning a remotely controlled aircraft which could be used to bomb a target. The leaders in the field were Orville Wright, who flew the first airplane, E. A. Sperry of the Sperry Gyroscope Company, and Charles F. Kettering of General Motors Corporation. It was these men who devised and tested the first missile, a small version of the aircraft used in those days. Although the first missile did not get into combat, a most important result of these early tests was the recommendation that any future work should be done with radio-controlled aircraft, so that the missile could be be given necessary adjustments while in flight.

In 1924, funds were allocated for developing a missile using radio control. Numerous moderately successful flights were made during the 1920's with radio control. By 1932, however, the project had been listed in the files under frills and luxuries and had been closed because of lack of funds.

About 1935, two brothers named Good, amateur model airplane builders, built and flew a model plane that was remotely controlled by radio waves transmitted from the ground. These flights were the first completely radio-controlled flights on record.

Radio-controlled target planes were the first airborne remote-controlled aircraft used by the U. S. Army and Navy.

By December of 1941, just before the U. S. entry into World War II, remote-controlled aircraft were developed to the point where they were seriously considered for use as a weapon of warfare by General H. H. Arnold, then Chief of Staff of the Army Air Corps.

So far this discussion has covered only missiles powered by internal combustion engines and propellers. Work also was done to develop missiles using reaction-type engines, including rocket engines, which contain within themselves all the elements needed for power, and jet engines, which depend on the surrounding atmosphere as a source of oxygen. When an atomic power plant for aircraft is developed, both the jet and rocket engines may become obsolete insofar as missile power plants are concerned.

Dr. Robert H. Goddard, at one time a physics professor at Clark University, Worcester, Massachusetts, was largely responsible for the sudden interest in rockets back in the twenties. When Dr. Goddard first started his experiments with rockets, no related technical information was available. He started a new science, industry, and field of engineering. Through his scientific experiments, he pointed the way to the development of rockets as we know them today. The Smithsonian Institute agreed to finance his experiments in 1920. From these experiments he wrote a paper titled "A Method of Reaching Extreme Altitudes," in which he outlined a space rocket of the step (multistage) principle, theoretically capable of reaching the moon.

Dr. Goddard discovered that with a properly shaped, smooth, tapered nozzle he could increase the ejection velocity eight times with the same weight of fuel. This would not only drive a rocket eight times faster, but sixty-four times farther, according to his theory. Early in his experiments he found that solid-fuel rockets would not give him the highly dependable supersonic motor capable of extreme altitudes. On 16 March 1926, after many trials, Dr. Goddard successfully fired, for the first time in history, a liquid-fuel rocket into the air. It attained an altitude of 184 feet and a speed of 60 mph. This seems small compared to present-day speeds and heights of missile flights, but instead of trying to achieve speed or altitude at this time, Dr. Goddard was trying to develop a dependable rocket motor.

Dr. Goddard later was the first to fire a rocket that reached a speed faster than the speed of sound. He was first to develop a gyroscopic steering apparatus for rockets. He was the first to use vanes in the jet stream for rocket stabilization during the initial phase of a rocket flight. He was also first to patent the idea of step rockets. After proving on paper and in actual tests that a rocket can travel in a vacuum, he developed the mathematical theory of rocket propulsion and rocket flight, including basic designs for long-range rockets. All of this information was available to U.S. military men before World War II, but evidently its immediate use did not seem applicable. Near the end of World War II the U. S. started intense work on rocket-powered guided missiles, using the experiments and developments of Dr. Goddard and the American Rocket Society.

The American Rocket Society began developing rockets and rocket motors after its organization in 1930. Its first motor was based mostly on German designs obtained from the German Rocket Society in 1931. The American Rocket Society was first to build a sectional rocket motor that could test motors of different sizes and shapes, thus cutting down the cost of a new motor for each type tested.

In 1941 some members of the American Rocket Society formed a company now known as Reaction Motors, Inc. It was organized to develop and manufacture rocket motors for both military and civilian use.

The first flight of a liquid-fuel rocket in Europe occurred in Germany on 14 March 1931, five years after Dr. Goddard made his first successful test with liquid fuel. A German scientist named Winkler was in charge. Winkler lost his life a short time later during one of his experiments.

Germany by this time had begun to sense the future importance of liquid-fuel rockets in warfare. In 1932 General Walter Dornberger (then a captain) of the German army obtained the necessary approval to develop liquid-fuel rockets for war purposes. By 1936, Germany decided to make research and development of guided missiles a major project. Germany spent $40,000,000 on a project, known as the "Peenemünde Project," for establishing a large rocket research and development laboratory. Hitler put the members of the German Rocket Society to work there, closing to the rest of the world German developments on rockets until after the war. Unlike Germany, the U. S. during this time paid little attention to the development of jet and rocket propulsion for any specific purpose.

(When you have filled in the headings, turn to page 243.)

*Example 3.*

No. That is not right. These are scrambled. The underlined heading never precedes the capitalized heading—and having the centered heading (which is the most important of all) following a capitalized heading is worse still.

Review the schedule of the headings on page 225, and then make the correct selection on page 233.

Your headings should look something like the ones shown on the following pages. Did you catch on that pages 239–241 are based on part of the outline of Panel 4–3? If you did, then you had no trouble making up headings. If you didn't realize this, or if your headings are markedly different from those shown on pages 244–246, look again at Panel 4–3 (page 227), and see for yourself that the outline is the best place to obtain your headings.

When you have finished checking your work, go to page 247.

## HISTORY OF ROCKETS

Just as World War II was not fought along the same lines as World War I, victory in a future war will not be realized by World War II aircraft practices. However, the solution of guided missile problems of the future will stem from past experiences. If anyone is to profit from the lessons learned from the missiles of the past, these lessons must be analyzed and applied in the light of the current situation.

## BIRTH OF GUIDED MISSILES

### World War I

The idea of guided missiles was born during World War I. The use of the airplane as a military weapon brought about considerable thought concerning a remotely controlled aircraft which could be used to bomb a target. The leaders in the field were Orville Wright, who flew the first airplane; E. A. Sperry of the Sperry Gyroscope Company; and Charles F. Kettering of General Motors Corporation. It was these men who devised and tested the first missile, a small version of the aircraft used in those days. Although the first missile did not get into combat, a most important result of these early tests was the recommendation that any future work should be done with radio-controlled aircraft, so that the missile could be given necessary adjustments while in flight.

### Post-War Developments

In 1924, funds were allocated for developing a missile using radio control. Numerous, moderately successful flights were made during the 1920's with radio control. By 1932, however, the project had been listed in the files under frills and luxuries and had been closed because of lack of funds.

About 1935, two brothers named Good, amateur model airplane builders, built and flew a model plane that was remotely controlled by radio waves transmitted from the ground. These flights were the first completely radio-controlled flights on record.

Radio-controlled target planes were the first airborne remote-controlled aircraft used by the U.S. Army and Navy.

### World War II

By December of 1941, just before the U.S. entry into World War II, remote-controlled aircraft were developed to the point where they were seriously considered for use as a weapon of warfare by General H. H. Arnold, then Chief of Staff of the Army Air Corps.

## Reaction-Type Engines

So far this discussion has covered only missiles powered by internal combustion engines and propellers. Work also was done to develop missiles using reaction-type engines, including rocket engines, which contain within themselves all the elements needed for power, and jet engines, which depend on the surrounding atmosphere as a source of oxygen. When an atomic power plant for aircraft is developed, both the jet and rocket engines may become obsolete insofar as missile power plants are concerned.

## AMERICAN ROCKETRY

### Dr. Goddard's Contribution

Dr. Robert H. Goddard, at one time a physics professor at Clark University, Worcester, Massachusetts, was largely responsible for the sudden interest in rockets back in the twenties. When Dr. Goddard first started his experiments with rockets, no related technical information was available. He started a new science, industry, and field of engineering. Through his scientific experiments, he pointed the way to the development of rockets as we know them today. The Smithsonian Institute agreed to finance his experiments in 1920. From these experiments he wrote a paper titled "A Method of Reaching Extreme Altitudes," in which he outlined a space rocket of the step (multistage) principle, theoretically capable of reaching the moon.

### Early Experiments

Dr. Goddard discovered that with a properly shaped, smooth, tapered nozzle he could increase the ejection velocity eight times with the same weight of fuel. This would not only drive a rocket eight times faster, but sixty-four times farther, according to his theory. Early in his experiments he found that solid-fuel rockets would not give him the highly dependable supersonic motor capable of extreme altitudes. On 16 March 1926, after many trials, Dr. Goddard successfully fired, for the first time in history, a liquid-fuel rocket into the air. It attained an altitude of 184 feet and a speed of 60 mph. This seems small compared to present-day speeds and heights of missile flights, but instead of trying to achieve speed or altitude at this time, Dr. Goddard was trying to develop a dependable rocket motor.

### Later Modifications

Dr. Goddard later was the first to fire a rocket that reached a speed greater than the speed of sound. He was first to develop a gyroscopic steering apparatus for rockets. He was the first to use vanes in the jet stream for rocket stabilization during the initial phase of a rocket flight.

He was also first to patent the idea of step rockets. After proving on paper and in actual tests that a rocket can travel in a vacuum, he developed the mathematical theory of rocket propulsion and rocket flight, including basic designs for long-range rockets. All of this information was available to U.S. military men before World War II, but evidently its immediate use did not seem applicable. Near the end of World War II the U.S. started intense work on rocket-powered guided missiles, using the experiments and developments of Dr. Goddard and the American Rocket Society.

## American Rocket Society

The American Rocket Society began developing rockets and rocket motors after its organization in 1930. Its first motor was based mostly on German designs obtained from the German Rocket Society in 1931. The American Rocket Society was first to build a sectional rocket motor that could test motors of different sizes and shapes, thus cutting down the cost of a new motor for each type tested.

In 1941 some members of the American Rocket Society formed a company now known as Reaction Motors, Inc. It was organized to develop and manufacture rocket motors for both military and civilian use.

## GERMAN ROCKETRY

The first flight of a liquid-fuel rocket in Europe occurred in Germany on 14 March 1931, five years after Dr. Goddard made his first successful test with liquid fuel. A German scientist named Winkler was in charge. Winkler lost his life a short time later during one of his experiments.

## Peenemünde Project

Germany by this time had begun to sense the future importance of liquid-fuel rockets in warfare. In 1932 General Walter Dornberger (then a captain) of the German army obtained the necessary approval to develop liquid-fuel rockets for war purposes. By 1936, Germany decided to make research and development of guided missiles a major project. Germany spent $40,000,000 on a project, known as the "Peenemünde Project," for establishing a large rocket research and development laboratory. Hitler put the members of the German Rocket Society to work there, closing to the rest of the world German developments on rockets until after the war. Unlike Germany, the U.S. during this time paid little attention to the development of jet and rocket propulsion for any specific purpose.

(Turn to page 247.)

If you write a report in which you refer your reader back and forth between paragraphs, you will want to identify your headings in some way. There are many ways of doing this, but we'll stick to just two. Remember the skeleton outline? Well, you can use the same identifications for your headings. It works this way.

SECTION I

TITLE

A.  MAJOR HEADING

1.  <u>Second-Level Heading</u>

a.  Third-Level Heading

B.  MAJOR HEADING

1.  <u>Second-Level Heading</u>

2.  <u>Second-Level Heading</u>

a.  Third-Level Heading

b.  Third-Level Heading

and so on.

If you need a fourth-level heading, it stands alone without a number or letter to mark it. You send your reader back or forth this way:

The organizational structure of the Purchasing Department allows flexibility in the purchase order system (paragraph II, A, 1, b). The manufacturing department, however, has a different structure, which is designed to suit its specific needs (paragraph II, B, 2, a).

Another convenient numbering system is the decimal style. Again we ask you to think back to the section on outlining. The decimal style of outlining can be used intact for numbering headings, as shown on the next page.

*(Continued on page 248.)*

SECTION I
TITLE

1. 1     MAIN HEADING

1. 1. 1    Second-Level Heading

1. 1. 1. 1    Third-Level Heading

1. 2     MAIN HEADING

1. 2. 1    Second-Level Heading

1. 2. 2    Second-Level Heading

1. 2. 2. 1    Third-Level Heading

In Section 2, the first number of every paragraph would be a 2, like this: 2.1.1 In Section 3, it would be a 3, and so on. Paragraph referencing under this system is easy. Here's a sample.

As previously described (paragraph 2.1.2.2), the klystron tuning procedure is a delicate one. The test equipment listed in paragraph 3.1 is required during the tuning procedure.

An important rule to remember when assigning headings and heading numbers is: you must have more than one of any given heading level in a section. We violated our own rule above, in order to show you its application. Paragraph 1.1.1 must be followed at some point by paragraph 1.1.2; otherwise you don't give paragraph 1.1.1 a number. In other words, you assign a number only to a paragraph that is followed by one or more additional paragraphs on the same level.

Go on to Chapter 5, page 251.

# 5

# Presentation of Data

Up to this point, we have talked about nothing but words. Illustrations, too, can be of great value, and you should be aware of their uses and their limitations. The illustrations you include in your report should do one of two jobs:

1. Give a picture, either a photograph or an artist's drawing, of how something actually looks.
2. Present data in an organized, easily understood form, by the use of lists, tables, charts, and graphs.

Let's look at the pictorial function first. The first rule we learn is a very serious limitation: we cannot use photographs or drawings with shaded areas. Because of reproduction cost, all the illustrations in your informal and semiformal reports must be in "line" form. That is, they must be rendered in black and white—the solid black of a printed line, and the solid white of unprinted paper. Panel 5–1 (next page) is a line drawing.

Right now, pick up a newspaper or magazine, and look at one of the printed photographs. Look closely—use a magnifying glass if you have one. As you see, the picture contains a pattern of dots. As the size of the dots varies, so does the shade of "gray" that is printed. This is the *halftone* process, which makes possible the reproduction of a full range of gray shades by means of the same elements used in a line drawing—black ink and white paper. The process is much too expensive, however, for any but full-scale formal reports. It involves photographing the original picture through a screen to create the dot pattern, and then printing the report on a regular printing press. The mimeograph and ditto machines that are used to reproduce the great majority of informal and semiformal reports simply can't do the job.

*(Continued on page 252.)*

You are writing a 10-page report that will be directed to management personnel, describing the operation of a new piece of machinery. You want to provide an illustration of the new machine. What is your most practical approach?

1. Use a photograph from the operator's manual that came with the machine. **Page 260**
2. Draw a picture yourself, similar to Panel 5–1. **Page 264**
3. Have an artist prepare a pencil drawing, with shading. **Page 266**

**PANEL 5–1**

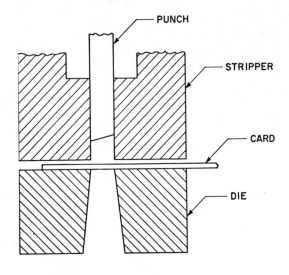

PUNCHING DEVICE

*Table, list, list, table.*

No, we disagree with you about Number 3, the sex, height, weight and age of employees.

Let's look at it again. We want to present four items of information about each of *x* number of employees (maybe a thousand). We know of three ways to present information: the paragraph, the list, and the table. We would hardly want to use an endless series of paragraphs, of course, and a list would be suitable for presenting only one column of data. The only possible choice is the table, probably set up like this:

### EMPLOYEE STATISTICS

| Name | Sex | Height | Weight | Age |
|------|-----|--------|--------|-----|
| Allen, James | M | 6'4" | 160 | 22 |
| Arney, Martha | F | 5'3" | 115 | 31 |
| . | . | . | . | . |
| . | . | . | . | . |
| . | . | . | . | . |

Go back to page 265 and select the correct answer.

## PANEL 5–2

| CITY | 1960 | 1950 |
|---|---|---|
| NEW YORK, N.Y. | 7,781,984 | 7,891,957 |
| CHICAGO, ILL. | 3,550,404 | 3,620,962 |
| LOS ANGELES, CALIF. | 2,479,015 | 1,970,358 |
| PHILADELPHIA, PA. | 2,002,505 | 2,071,665 |
| DETROIT, MICH. | 1,670,114 | 1,849,568 |
| BALTIMORE, MD. | 939,024 | 949,708 |
| HOUSTON, TEXAS | 938,219 | 596,163 |
| CLEVELAND, OHIO | 876,050 | 914,808 |
| WASHINGTON, D.C. | 763,956 | 802,178 |
| ST. LOUIS, MO. | 750,026 | 856,796 |

MAJOR U.S. CITIES AND THEIR POPULATIONS
TABLE I

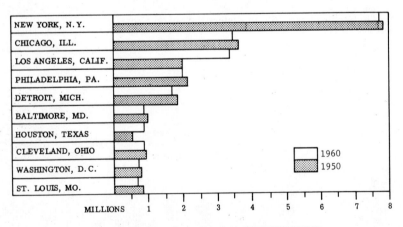

FIGURE 1. MAJOR U.S. CITIES AND THEIR POPULATIONS

BAR CHART

*Table, list, table, table.*

Right. That was a pretty easy question, wasn't it? You should never have any trouble choosing among paragraph, list, and table. Your data makes the choice for you.

We come now to the last important type of visual data presentation, charts and graphs. A table organizes data into columns and rows, but it relies on the typewriter for the actual presentation. Charts and graphs, on the other hand, use bars, lines, maps, stick figures—the only limitations on the sophistication of the art work are imagination and budget.

We will use the terms "chart" and "graph" interchangeably. Some people like to distinguish between them, and, indeed, distinctions once existed: a chart was a map of a geographical area, and a graph presented data (in math, an equation was expressed on a graph). But today the words have lost their distinctive meanings.

Panel 5–2 (opposite page) contains the same data expressed in two ways, by table and by chart (or graph, as you prefer). Examine them both. Then, in a sentence or two, tell us under what circumstances a table would be preferable, and when you would be better advised to use a chart.

Go to page 257.

*Table, paragraph, table, table.*

You're right about all except Number 2, the personnel available for overseas assignment. You *could* use a paragraph to present the names of the available personnel, but we should ask ourselves, is this the best available method? We think not. Which is easier to read, a list of names, or a series of names in a paragraph? We think you'll agree on second thought that a list is the better form.

Go back to page 265 and make another selection.

See if you agree with us: We say that a table is the better tool when you want to present exact quantities, and a chart is better if you want to present comparisons. Thus, it would be very hard to create a chart so accurate that the person using it could read the exact population of New York, 7,781,984. But the bar chart dramatizes much more effectively the variations in size between the 10 cities.

Of course, you can have your cake and eat it, too, if you use the chart form and also enter the exact quantity in or near the appropriate bar, as in Panel 5–3.

Panel 5–4 (pages 258–259) illustrates seven common types of charts and graphs. Study them carefully. Note that they all present a picture of a situation. In each case, consider the amount of time, effort, and space that would be required if the information had to be presented by words alone.

Go to page 261.

**PANEL 5–3**

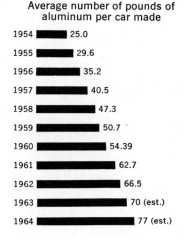

Average number of pounds of
aluminum per car made

|  | |
|------|------|
| 1954 | 25.0 |
| 1955 | 29.6 |
| 1956 | 35.2 |
| 1957 | 40.5 |
| 1958 | 47.3 |
| 1959 | 50.7 |
| 1960 | 54.39 |
| 1961 | 62.7 |
| 1962 | 66.5 |
| 1963 | 70 (est.) |
| 1964 | 77 (est.) |

**PANEL 5-4**

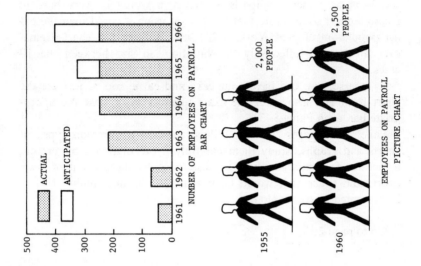

NUMBER OF EMPLOYEES ON PAYROLL
BAR CHART

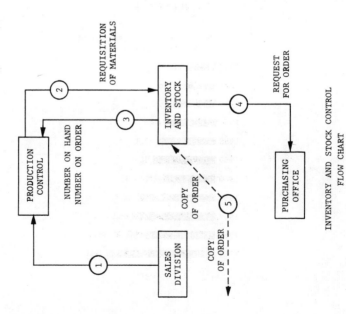

EMPLOYEES ON PAYROLL
PICTURE CHART

INVENTORY AND STOCK CONTROL
FLOW CHART

PRESIDENT

MANUFACTURING MANAGER

ENGINEERING CHIEF ENGINEER

SALES MANAGER

ACCOUNTING CHIEF ACCOUNTANT

FACTORY

PRODUCTION CONTROL

EASTERN SALES DISTRICT

SERVICE DIVISION

WESTERN SALES DISTRICT

TYPICAL CORPORATION STRUCTURE
ORGANIZATION CHART

50% SALARIES

20% CAPITAL

20% EXPANSION

10% STOCK-HOLDERS

WHERE THE MONEY GOES
PIE CHART

DOLLARS

800

600

400

200

0

J F M A M J J A S

EXPENSES

RECEIPTS

RECEIPTS & EXPENSES (BY MONTH)
LINE CHART

VT

NH

MASS

RI

CONN

NEW YORK

NEW JERSEY

PENNA

SALES OFFICE LOCATIONS
MAP

*Use a photograph from the operator's manual that came with the machine.*

No, you're not making the most practical approach. First let's decide what kind of report we will write on this assignment. It's to be 10 pages long, with distribution within the company. Doesn't that make it semiformal? And we said that photographs were just too expensive to appear in a semiformal report.

Go back to page 252 and make another selection.

One thing you've probably noticed is that charts and graphs are more difficult to create, and therefore more expensive, than tables. But they are usually more effective. It's up to you to weigh the factors of expense and effectiveness of presentation to see how many, if any, charts and graphs you can use.

Once you've made this decision, you can use any of the seven types pictured in Panel 5–4. Frequently two or more types will accomplish the same job; for instance, we expressed the "Number of Employees on Payroll" in both bar chart and picture chart format. Another chance for you to make a decision. Maybe a technical audience would feel more at home with a bar chart, and a nontechnical group would be happier with a picture chart.

Assume you are writing a formal report for wide distribution outside the company. Among other points, you want to (1) describe the way in which investors' money is spent, (2) give the profit figures for each of the past five years, and (3) show how the company is organized. Which type of chart would best do each job?

**1.** Bar chart, bar chart, organization chart.    **Page 267**
**2.** Pie chart, bar chart, organization chart.    **Page 268**
**3.** Line chart, bar chart, picture chart.    **Page 262**

**262**

*Line chart, bar chart, picture chart.*

Well, you're right about the bar chart, but that's all! A line chart would not be suitable for showing the ways in which the investor dollar is split up. (Try to draw one up—what purpose would the line serve?) And how would a picture chart be used to show the company organization? Look again (carefully this time) at Panel 5–4, pages 258–259, then make another selection on page 261.

We're confident that you selected the flow chart as the best to use in graphically representing a production process. It's the only possible selection—a classic case of the data selecting its own best method of presentation.

Now go on to page 271.

*Draw a picture yourself, similar to Panel 5–1.*

Right. You may hesitate to rely on your artistic talents, but this is the most practical approach. The report will be semiformal (10 pages long, directed within the company), which disqualifies the photograph. And as for the artist's drawing, not only is his time expensive, but, because of the shaded gray areas, the pencil drawing is just as expensive to reproduce as a photo.

So the point to remember is this: in all but the formal report, rely on line drawings, and, unless your budget is generous, do them yourself. This takes a little skill. Depending on the reproduction process available to you, you may have to draw your picture on a ditto or mimeograph master, which isn't as easy as drawing on a sheet of paper. But with a little practice, you'll do surprisingly well.

So much for pictures. Now we come to the second category of illustrations, those that present data. You will probably have numerous occasions to use these techniques. Watch for opportunities and use visual presentation whenever possible. Data can be presented in lists, in tables, and in charts and graphs. The method you employ depends on the information you wish to convey, and your audience.

Let's define our terms. This is a list:

### CHEMICAL ELEMENTS

> Actinium
> Aluminum
> Americium
> Antimony
> Argon
> Arsenic
> Barium

Information is listed when it is desirable to have each item stand alone for easier understanding. Lists are typewritten, and contain no art work.

*(Continued on page 265.)*

This is a table:

### CHEMICAL ELEMENTS

| Element | Symbol | Atomic Number | Atomic Weight | Year Discovered | Discoverer |
|---------|--------|---------------|---------------|-----------------|------------|
| Actinium | Ac | 89 | 227 | 1899 | Debierne |
| Aluminum | Al | 13 | 26.98 | 1825 | Oersted |
| Americium | Am | 95 | 243 | 1944 | Seaborg, *et al.* |
| Antimony | Sb | 51 | 121.76 | 1450 | Valentine |
| Argon | Ar | 18 | 39.944 | 1894 | Rayleigh, Ramsay |

A table is any presentation of data that is read across as well as down. It is typewritten, and does not contain art work. It imposes a logical order on data, makes for easy comparison, and saves space. Consider how much easier this table is to read than a series of paragraphs would be. Although tables are often ruled, they do not have to be. A typist can prepare a table with only slightly more effort than she uses in typing a paragraph.

Would you use a list, a table, or a paragraph to present the following groups of data?

1. A comparison of prices of three items for the last five years.
2. The names of personnel available for overseas assignment.
3. Height, sex, weight, and age of employees.
4. Parcel post rates to various cities, for packages of various weights.

**1.** Table, list, list, table.  **Page 253**
**2.** Table, list, table, table.  **Page 255**
**3.** Table, paragraph, table, table.  **Page 256**

*Have an artist prepare a pencil drawing, with shading.*

Well, that isn't a really bad answer, but it isn't right, either. We have reservations on two counts:

1. Who's the artist? You're assuming that you have one available. It's possible that you will, but not entirely likely. Also, his time costs money. You'll find that the most practical approach is usually the cheapest.

2. We didn't tell you this before, but the sad truth is that a pencil drawing with shading is just as hard—and expensive—to reproduce as a photograph (because of those gray shaded areas). So remember—unless your report is formal, you *must* stick with line drawings.

Go back to page 252 and make another selection.

*Bar chart, bar chart, organization chart.*

Well, except for the fact that you're using a bar chart to show how investor money is spent, you did very well. That isn't a serious mistake; the information *could* be presented in bar-chart form. But the bar chart does not show the relationship between the amounts quite as clearly—and besides, we showed you an example of a pie chart doing just this job.

Go back to page 261 and make another selection.

*Pie chart, bar chart, organization chart.*

Right you are. The main thing to remember about charts and graphs (and about lists and tables, too) is, as much as possible, to let the data choose its own best means of expression. Then, if there is still a choice between two or three methods, make the selection on the basis of your audience. Of course, your decision will also be influenced by who will actually draw the chart. Most likely you'll be the designer, and you'll want to choose the type of presentation that's easiest for you to turn out.

Now let's try one final exercise: Which of the seven types of charts illustrated in Panel 5–4 (pages 258–259) would best illustrate the various stages in a production process, from raw material to finished product?

Check your answer on page 263.

6

# Informational Reports

In Chapter 2 we classified reports by format, and you learned to distinguish between informal, semiformal, and formal reports. Now we'll classify reports in another way: by the job they do. Thus we have informational, analytical, and special purpose reports, and each of these categories includes a couple of subgroups. When you have decided what type of report you are writing (for instance, informal analytical, or semiformal informational) you will have a very good idea of how much to write, and, equally important, which parts of the general report format to include.

Let's talk about informational reports first. They come in three varieties:

1. *Progress reports,* which relate changes in conditions over a period of time.

2. *Status reports,* which describe conditions at a specific moment in time.

3. *Narrative reports,* which describe an event.

All three types have in common the fact that they present information, but make no effort to evaluate the information or to make recommendations. Their role is purely informative.

Which of the following situations would be treated in an informational report?

1. A discussion of the results of a time and motion study.
**Page 277**
2. A monthly report of the activities of the Sales Department.
**Page 274**
3. A proposal which suggests the best procedure to follow in a company reorganization.    **Page 280**

*Outline 1 is a progress-to-date report; Outline 3 is a periodical report.*

Very good. You've got the picture on progress reports.

The second kind of informational report that we mentioned is the status report. The progress report deals with a period of time; the status report deals with a moment in time. It describes conditions *as of a given date.* Therefore, its format will be quite simple: a very brief introduction, perhaps a summary, the body, and in a few cases, conclusions and appendix material. Conclusions are rare and recommendations nonexistent in the status report because, like the progress report, it doesn't analyze data or recommend future actions. Just as you compare the periodical report to a newspaper story, and the progress-to-date report to a history book, think of a status report as being like your monthly bank statement: it tells you *how things are on a given day.*

Which of the following are status reports?

1. A report on the number and type of ships in New York harbor on April 1st.

2. A report on the completion of a project, including date of completion and summary of windup activities.

3. A list of your expenditures for the month of March.

4. A report describing damage suffered by one of the company delivery trucks in a traffic accident.

**1.** Numbers 1 and 2 are status reports.     **Page 273**
**2.** Numbers 1 and 4 are status reports.     **Page 281**
**3.** Numbers 2 and 3 are status reports.     **Page 278**
**4.** All of them are status reports.     **Page 283**

*Numbers 1 and 2 are status reports.*

Well, you're half right. That report about the ships *is* a status report (the date was a dead giveaway). But the one on the completion of a project includes "a summary of windup activities." Those activities must have occurred over a period of time. Is that consistent with our definition of a status report?

Go back to page 272 and make another selection.

*A monthly report of the activities of the Sales Department.*

Right. That's a good example of an informational report. In fact, as you may have noticed, it's a perfect example of a progress report: it relates changes in conditions over a period of time.

There are two kinds of progress reports, which differ according to the length of time they cover. The "periodical" report concerns itself with a fixed period—a week, or a month. It is directly comparable to the "Review of the Week's Events" that appears in your Sunday paper. It is usually short, and, since it is in effect a news story, it will generally contain only an introduction, perhaps a brief summary, and the body of information. Conclusions and appendixes will be needed only very rarely, and recommendations, of course, never. A longer form of the progress report describes "progress to date" by tracing the history of a project from the beginning right up to the present. It can cover a period of time ranging up to several years, and can therefore be very long and involved. Any of the parts of the general report format may be included, except recommendations—once again, remember that the progress report deals with time in the past.

*(Continued on page 275.)*

Which kinds of reports are represented by the following outlines?

1. I. Introduction
   II. Summary
   III. Discussion
      A. Early Stages
      B. Research and Development
      C. Production Stage
      D. Phasing Out

2. I. Introduction
   II. Body
      A. This week in the Paint Shop
      B. This week in the Repair Shop
   III. Summary
   IV. Recommendations

3. I. Introduction
   II. Summary
   III. Body—record of inventory depletion for March.

**1.** Outline 1 is a progress-to-date report; Outlines 2 and 3 are periodical reports.   **Page 276**
**2.** Outlines 1 and 3 are periodical reports; Outline 2 is a progress-to-date report.   **Page 279**
**3.** Outline 1 is a progress-to-date report; Outline 3 is a periodical report.   **Page 272**

*Outline 1 is a progress-to-date report; Outlines 2 and 3 are periodical reports.*

No, you missed that one. You're partly right: Outline 1 is a progress-to-date report, and Outline 3 is a periodical report. But what about Outline 2? The last item in that one is "IV. Recommendations." Didn't we say that progress reports *never* make recommendations?

Go back to page 275 and make another selection.

*A discussion of the results of a time and motion study.*

No, that isn't right. A discussion would necessarily involve the evaluation of data—considerably more than the simple presentation that would appear in an informational report. If this seems to you like splitting hairs, let us say that it is done only to emphasize the point that informational reports contain *nothing but information.*

Go back to page 271 and select the correct answer.

**278**

*Numbers 2 and 3 are status reports.*

No, you didn't do too well on that one. Neither one of those is a status report. Let's reconsider: The report on the completion of a project contained a "summary of windup activities." Those activities must have taken place over a period of at least a few days, and thus the report can't be a status report. As for the list of expenditures during March, unless you spent all your money on the same day, you must be talking about a period of time. Again by our definition, this can't be a status report.

Go back to page 272 and make another selection.

*Outlines 1 and 3 are periodical reports; Outline 2 is a progress-to-date report.*

No, you're not clear yet on the differences between periodical and progress-to-date reports. Look at Outline 1. Does that look like a weekly or monthly report? Remember, a periodical report reads like a newspaper story; a progress-to-date report reads more like a history book. Outline 3 is obviously a periodical report, but you're completely wrong about Outline 2. How could a report that twice uses the word "week" be called progress-to-date, considering the definition we used?

Reread page 274 and make the correct selection on page 275.

*A proposal which suggests the best procedure to follow in a company reorganization.*

No, you're wrong. A proposal suggests—makes recommendations —and we said that informational reports do not make recommendations. In fact, they never deal with the future at all. Informational reports relate events that occurred in the past, and that's all they do.

Go back to page 271 and choose again.

*Numbers 1 and 4 are status reports.*

Right. Very good. Those are the ones that describe conditions at a moment in time. Just remember that if there's a hint of time passing, you won't be using a status report.

Go to page 282.

So far, we've learned about two kinds of progress reports (the periodical and the progress-to-date) and the status report. The last kind of informational report is the narrative, which is like the progress report in that it tells a story, but unlike it in that there is no reference to time. The periodical report has 7-day or 30-day limitations. The progress-to-date report relates events up to the present. On the other hand, the narrative report tells a story that could have happened any time. It doesn't necessarily deal with changes in conditions, or conditions at any given moment. Any of the parts of the general report format may be present, with the exception of recommendations. As we said, recommendations imply analysis of data, and informational reports don't analyze.

Which of the following would be a narrative report?

1. A company's annual report to stockholders.     **Page 285**
2. A description of a building the company is thinking of renting—dimensions, condition of building and facilities, etc. **Page 293**
3. An executive's report on a business trip to six company subsidiaries.     **Page 287**

*All of them are status reports.*

We think you're guessing. But, guessing or not, you're half right. The question is, which half? Remember: a status report describes conditions at a *moment* in time. If there's any suggestion that the events covered in a report occurred over a period of days or weeks, that report is not a status report.

Now let's try it again. Which are the status reports?

1. A report on the number and type of ships in New York harbor on April 1st.

2. A report on the completion of a project, including date of completion and summary of windup activities.

3. A list of your expenditures for the month of March.

4. A report describing damage suffered by one of the company delivery trucks in a traffic accident.

1. Numbers 1 and 2.    **Page 292**
2. Numbers 1 and 4.    **Page 286**
3. Numbers 2 and 3.    **Page 284**

*Numbers 2 and 3.*

You're getting worse—this time you're not even half right. Now we know you were guessing back there on page 272.

This really isn't a difficult idea, so let's concentrate on it and get it right. Status reports describe conditions at *one point in time*. They *don't* concern themselves with changes in conditions, but report things as they are *on a given date*. The report described in Example 2 contains a "summary of windup activities." These activities must have occurred over a period of time, and therefore the report can't be of the "status" variety. The list of expenditures for the month of March in Example 3 must be itemized by date. Again, time passes, and it can't be a status report. (A statement of cash on hand at month's end would be.) Got it now?

Go back to page 283 and make the correct selection.

*A company's annual report to stockholders.*

Wrong! We're surprised you missed that one, after all we said about progress reports and their associated time limitation. Doesn't an annual report describe changes in conditions over a fixed period of time? So what else could it be but a periodical report?

Go back and review from page 271.

*Numbers 1 and 4.*

Right you are. Good. You have the idea—if time passes, it isn't a status report. Now let's turn to the last kind of informational report.

Go to page 282.

*An executive's report on a business trip to six company subsidiaries.*

Very good. That one meets the requirements of the narrative report—it relates a series of events without any time limitations. The trip might have taken place last week, or a couple of months ago.

Panels 6–1 through 6–4, starting on page 288, contain examples of the four types of informational reports we've covered, with their parts in scrambled order. Identify each one according to type, and prepare an outline of each report, with the sections in the correct order according to the general report format. Then compare your answers with the ones on page 294.

## PANEL 6–1

Discussion
     The system as finally installed was changed
in a couple of respects from the plans originally
proposed by the contractor...
     The result of these changes was a small in-
crease in our cost, which breaks down as
follows:...
     Our consulting engineer, Bob Haskins, says
that his preliminary inspection reveals no causes
for complaint...
     We talked to about 30 of the 103 workers in
the area, and they were enthusiastic about the
system...

Appendix
     Attached are copies of contractor's bills for
the items not included in the original proposal.

Introduction
     The installation of air conditioning in the
west wing was undertaken last April 15 by Morgan
and Hartley Engineering Co., whose original price
was $16,000. Progress on the job is described in
reports from this office dated June 1, July 9, and
September 3...

Summary
     The installation of the new air conditioning
system in the west wing is complete as of the date
of this report. Final cost was $16,676. Small
changes were made in the original plans. The
system is working fine, and initial employee reaction is entirely favorable.

Conclusions
     The new air conditioning installation in the
west wing seems entirely satisfactory.

## PANEL 6–2

Summary
    The research staff has been investigating the
feasibility of adding a new type of watercolor
pad to our line.  Originally intended as a one-
man, 6-month study, the program was begun last
January.  As of June 1, it is only 40% complete
because...

Conclusions
    Progress has been slower than anticipated...

Introduction
    Our line now includes only one type of water-
color paper, our #6904, which is a light, porous,
cheap sheet.  Both our principal competitors offer
at least two grades.  The purpose of this investigation was (a) to determine the best type of paper
to add, (b) to select a supplier, and (c) to come
up with an estimated cost for the project...

Discussion
    The selection of a paper that would be com-
petitive in price and quality with those already
in the field proved to be much more difficult than
anticipated.  None of the mills that currently
supply us wanted to attempt to meet our specifi-
cations, and it was necessary to approach several
with whom we had no previous dealings...
    The mills we approached were...
    By the first of March we still had not been
able to settle upon the most suitable formula...
    On April 10 we contacted the West Fork Paper
Co., which seemed eager to enter into an agreement
with us on our terms...
    West Fork could not measure up to our stand-
ards, and negotiations were broken off...
    The cost figures are still not final, as we
haven't settled on either a formula or a supplier.

290

**PANEL 6–3**

To:          C. Conklin, Division Mgr.
From:        F. Franklin, Repair Shop Supervisor
Re:          Weekly Progress Report

Discussion
    Of the 14 men in the shop, 6 are still work-
ing on the repairs to the fluorescent tube shaper.
Work on this job is now 85% complete, as compared
to 50% at the end of last week. Three men are
rebuilding burned-out FQ-6 transformers. This
work, started Tuesday, is 50% complete. Three
men are on loan to the tube division in Building 4,
repairing a broken-down transistor-fabricating
machine. The work there began Wednesday and is 70%
complete as of Friday. One man is helping me with
miscellaneous small repairs here in the shop. The
last man is on vacation. No time was lost this
week due to sickness or accident. The new man,
Miller, hired Dec. 15, is working in very nicely
and seems to be a valuable addition to the crew.

Introduction
    This report describes the activities of the
Equipment Repair Shop, Building 6, Norton Elec-
tronics Co., Weedville Division, for the week
Jan. 13-Jan. 20.

Conclusions
    Work is progressing smoothly on all jobs.
There is no appreciable backlog. The only job
still waiting for attention is the rebuilding of
the motor of the forklift truck from the Raw
Materials Dept.

## PANEL 6–4

Summary

Our tour of neighborhoods for the purpose of
showing off the new model was conducted on April 5,
and was quite successful. We stopped in 17 areas;
crowds averaged about 75 people; and the tabulated
results of interviews showed that 85 percent of
those interviewed reacted favorable.     favorably.

Introduction

The experience of the past two years has
shown that neighborhood tours serve two definite
purposes:
1. They advertise the new model.
2. They give us a chance to sample public
reaction to the new model.
There were a couple of innovations on this
year's tour...

Discussion

The tour started at 7:00 at company headquarters. Our 10-man staff included...
The first stop was at the corner of Miller
and Maple Streets. The crowd here consisted
mainly of factory workers on their way to the
steel mill. Allowing for early-morning sleepi-
ness, their reaction was generally favorable.
The second stop was...
The third stop was..., etc.

Appendix

Breakdown of answers obtained in interviews.

Conclusions

Over-all acceptance was 85 percent favorable.
Of the remaining 15 percent, no single complaint
totaled more than 2 percent. Both the new model
and the tour itself were greeted enthusiastically.

*Numbers 1 and 2.*

No, you're still only half right. The report about ships in New York harbor on April 1st is obviously a status report. But the second one contains a "summary of windup activities." Don't you think that those activities occurred over a period of time? They must have, and therefore that can't be a status report.

Go back to page 272, read the material on status reports carefully, and then choose the right answer on page 283.

*A description of a building the company is thinking of renting—dimensions, condition of building and facilities, etc.*

No, this isn't a narrative report. Look again. When we describe the condition of the building and facilities, aren't we describing them as of right now, or at least as of the day on which we make our inspection? That makes this sound pretty much like a status report to us. What do you think?

Go back to page 282 and make another selection.

*Your work should look like this:*

Panel 6–1—Status report

    I. Introduction
    II. Summary
    III. Discussion
    IV. Conclusions
    V. Appendix

Panel 6–2—Progress-to-date report

    I. Introduction
    II. Summary
    III. Discussion
    IV. Conclusions

Panel 6–3—Periodical report (weekly)

    I. Introduction
    II. Body
    III. Conclusions

Panel 6–4—Narrative report

    I. Introduction
    II. Summary
    III. Discussion
    IV. Conclusions
    V. Appendix

If you missed identifying any of the types of informational reports, return to the following pages for review: progress report, page 274; status report, page 272; narrative report, page 282.

If you didn't get the sections of the reports in the right order, review report format in Chapter 2.

If your answers were perfect, good work. Go to page 297.

# 7

# Analytical Reports

The material which follows is slightly different in presentation from that of the preceding chapters. There won't be any skipping around—when you reach the bottom of one page, you'll go right on to the next.

On each page you will find several short consecutive items (or *frames*), set off from each other by dividing lines. For each frame, you are to fill in blanks (one word to a blank) or choose an answer; the correct response(s) will be shown below the line which marks the beginning of the following frame.

To use this material effectively, you need to provide yourself with a *mask* of paper or cardboard, about the size of this page. Use the mask to cover the page area below the frame you are working on. When you have completed that frame, move your mask down to uncover the correct response, and check your answer. If it was wrong, correct it. Then do the new frame. And so on.

Now—do you have your mask ready? As soon as you do, turn the page and begin with the first frame.

An analytical report is one in which the writer analyzes the facts or data and then presents conclusions and recommendations.

If your wife said something happened to the car today, you would

_____ her statement and draw your own conclusions.

---

*analyze*

As the result of analyzing your girlfriend's financial statement from

the bank, you would first draw some _____

then you would make some _____.

---

*conclusions, recommendations*

The pattern for analytical reports is:

1. _____ the facts;

2. draw _____ concerning the facts;

3. make your _____.

---

*analyze*
*conclusions*
*recommendations*

The conclusions and recommendations portions of an analytical report are the . . . [most/least] important part of the report. (Underline your choice).

*most*

Since the _____ and

_____ are so important, they will

usually come . . . [early/late] in the report.

---

*conclusions, recommendations, early*

Previously we taught you that the summary should come early in a

report. Do you think the summary should still come early in an analyt-

ical report? . . . [Yes/No]

---

*Yes.* (We must still summarize the report for the reader, and the earlier,
the better.)

Immediately following the summary of an analytical report, you

will find the writer's _____ and

_____.

---

*conclusions, recommendations*

You will easily be able to spot an analytical report because:

1. it will _____ the facts presented;

2. it will present _____
   drawn by the writer from the facts;

3. it will present _____ made
   by the writer based upon the facts presented;

4. it will usually have, following the _____, the

   writer's conclusions and recommendations.

*analyze*
*conclusions*
*recommendations*
*summary*

Analytical reports can be broken up into three general types:

1. the problem-solving type
2. the proposal type
3. the research type

You could expect some overlapping between the

_____ and the

_____ type of analytical report, but

you can readily see that the _____

type of analytical report will stand pretty much alone.

---

*problem-solving*
  (or *first*)
*proposal*
  (or *second*)
*research*
  (or *third*)

If the facts to be analyzed represent a highly troublesome area, the

analytical report would be of the _____

type.

---

*problem-solving*

In a problem-solving report the writer's solution would come in

the _____ portion of the report.

---

*recommendations*

An analytical report proposing that the assembly line be shifted to the north end of the plant, thereby saving $10,000, would qualify as a _____ type.

---

*proposal*

A proposal report _____ some new or future improvement or change.

---

*suggests* (or *recommends*)

An analytical report describing the research being done by the laboratory group on a new widget would be classified as a

_____ type of analytical report.

---

*research*

Research reports can be broken down into two subtypes: (1) basic research and (2) applied research.

A basic research report would be concerned with only the

_____ type of research.

---

*basic*

A report describing the design of a new type of transistor circuit would be a(an) _____ _____ report.

*basic research*

Since a basic research report describes a research effort, an applied research report would be concerned with how to _____ the new development.

---

*apply* (or *use*)

If you developed a radically new mousetrap you would write a(an) _____ _____ type of analytical report describing the research and design. To tell the sales manager how to use this new mousetrap you would write a(an) _____ _____ type of analytical report.

---

*basic research, applied research*

Since, when he is writing a basic research report, the writer is simply analyzing what took place, not evaluating what the new development can do, no _____ section is usually included in the report.

---

*recommendations*

Since an applied research report suggests ways of using new products or techniques it will contain, as a matter of course, both a _____ section and a _____ section.

*conclusions, recommendations*

A word of warning is in order. Your reports cannot always be neatly pigeonholed as one type or another. A report can fall into several of the classifications we have discussed, depending upon the approach the report writer wishes to take.

Go on to the next frame.

---

What are the three types of analytical reports?

_____

_____

_____

---

*problem-solving*
*proposal*
*research*

Describe how the analytical report differs from the informational report:

*The analytical report is written in order to break down (or analyze) an existing set of conditions, then make recommendations for the improvement of those conditions, if possible* (or some similar statement).

You are asked to investigate a project and describe the development of a new type of water pump. Your report analyzes why the pump's performance is below design standards and recommends changes in the company's design and development procedures.

What type of report is this?

1. problem-solving
2. proposal
3. basic research

*It can be any one of the following:*

1. *Problem-solving,* if you have been asked to tell why the performance is substandard and recommend a solution.
2. *Proposal,* if you have specifically suggested future changes in procedures or methods now in use.
3. *Basic research,* if you are reporting on a development of the pump as a routine report of new projects within the company.

Note that your report is of a different type each time, depending on *the purpose for which it is written.*

Go on to Chapter 8.

8

# Special Purpose Reports

Special purpose reports might be considered the "everything else" category because they contain elements found in both informational and analytical reports. For example, they may report progress *and* analyze why it has been either slow or fast.

A report that tells the history of a project, describes problems that have arisen, and suggests a solution to those problems would be a

_____    _____    _____.

---

*special purpose report*

Special purpose reports . . . [can/cannot] contain a conclusions and recommendations section.

---

*can*

A report that tells the history of a project, describes problems that progress to date, reasons for the present status, what will be done to improve matters, and suggestions for the future would be a

_____    _____ report.

---

*special purpose*

Three types of special purpose reports are commonly in use in scientific and engineering corporations: preliminary reports, interim reports, and final reports. These reports will not only report progress, but they will state what is anticipated on the project (preliminary or interim) or what the end results were (final).

Go on to the next frame.

When the Placebo Drug Co. began research to develop a new type of tranquilizer, the project chemist first submitted a(an) _____ report detailing an analysis of the problem, the project design, anticipated steps to achieve success, and a tentative end date for completion of the project.

---

*preliminary*

Halfway through, the project chemist put out a report describing progress to date and telling why the project was six weeks behind schedule. He also listed what he planned to do to speed up the pace of the project. This was a(an) _____ report.

---

*interim*

When the new drug had been safely tested on animals and was ready for a series of tests on humans, the project chemist published a(an) _____ report covering the entire project, from beginning to end, as well as his recommendations for the field tests of the drug.

---

*final*

The three types of special purpose reports commonly used are the _____, the _____, and the _____ reports.

---

*preliminary, interim, final*

    The special purpose report will not be informal in nature; therefore, you can say that it is restricted to the _____ and the _____ types of reports.

---

*semiformal* &#125; either order
*formal* 

    Describe the special purpose report.

---

*The special purpose report is a report that presents a summary, gives progress and status information, makes recommendations and yields conclusions, and predicts future conditions of a given stituation* (or some similar statement).

    Special purpose reports, because they usually cover a large subject or segment of a subject, will contain tables and graphs. In experimental reports, illustrations to show circuits, laboratory apparatus, etc., are almost mandatory. A report of the design and development of a new radio circuit will have _____ showing the new design features.

---

*illustrations,* (or *pictures,* or *schematics,* or *line drawings*)

Government agencies require that special purpose reports be submitted to them for all contracts. The rules you have learned about audience, method of writing, and language usage will apply to these reports. Your audience (the agency) will tell you what format you are to use.

Congratulations! You have just finished a programed course in how to write effective reports. We hope the knowledge you have gained will be useful to you in your future report writing.